D1312165

U.S. History Maps

By
DON BLATTNER

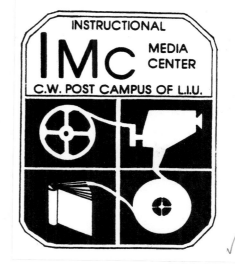

COPYRIGHT © 1999 Mark Twain Media, Inc.

ISBN 1–58037–109–4

Printing No. CD-1336

Mark Twain Media, Inc., Publishers
Distributed by Carson-Dellosa Publishing Company, Inc.

Table of Contents

Introduction iv
Before Humans Arrived
   Ice Age in North America 1
   Lake Agassiz 2
   Ice Age Definitions 3
The First Americans
   Discovering the Americas 4
   Route of the First Americans 5
   America's Earliest Settlers 6
   Map of Indian Tribes in the United States 7
European Exploration
   Viking Voyagers 8
   Viking Voyages Map Activity 9
   Christopher Columbus 10
   Columbus Quiz 11
   Voyages of Cabot and Vespucci 12
   The World as Known Before Columbus 13
   The World as Known in 1500 13
   Other Early Explorers 14
   Map of da Gama and Magellan Voyages 15
   Other Early Explorers Quiz 16
   Spanish Conquistadors 17
   Spanish Explorers Quiz 18
   Spanish Conquistadors Quiz 19
   French Explorers 20
   French Explorers Puzzle 21
   English Explorers 23
   Describing the Geographic Features of the United States 24
   Famous Explorers 25
   Who Gets the New World? 26
The Settling of America
   Settlements in the New World 27
   New Spain 27
   New Spain Quiz 28
   New France and New Netherlands 29
   New England 30
   Later English Colonies 31
   The Massachussets Bay Colony 32
   Countries That Colonized 33
   The English Colonies Grow 35
   Knowing the Original Colonies 36
Wars and Conflicts on the Continent
   The French and Indian War 37
   Map of the French and Indian War 38
   How Well Do You Know Canada? 39
   War of Independence 40
   Major Battles of the War for Independence Map 41

Table of Contents

Important Battles of the Revolutionary War 42

Patriots of the American Revolution 43

Separated by a Common Language 44

The War of 1812 45

War of 1812 Quiz 46

The Star-Spangled Banner 47

Florida Purchase From Spain in 1819 49

War With Mexico 50

War With Mexico Puzzle 53

America Grows

European Possession Changes in America 1664–1775 54

The United States in 1783 55

Are You From Virginia? 56

Indian Relocation: Trail of Tears 57

Indian Relocation: Points of View 58

Famous Native Americans 58

The Northwest Ordinance of 1787 59

Identify States Developed From the Northwest Territory 59

Louisiana Purchase 60

Identify States Developed From the Louisiana Purchase 61

The Lewis and Clark Expedition 62

Lewis and Clark Quiz 63

U.S. Growth Since 1783 64

Growth of the United States Quiz 65

Trails Leading Westward 66

Which Trail Would You Take? 67

Oregon Country 68

Oregon Country Puzzle 69

The Panama Canal 70

Panama Canal Quiz 71

Alaska 72

Hawaii 73

Identifying States by Their Shapes 74

Slavery in America

Slavery in America 76

The Missouri Compromise 77

The Compromise of 1850 77

The Kansas-Nebraska Act 78

Slavery Leads to War 79

Slavery Quiz 80

Transportation

Transcontinental Railroad 82

Transcontinental Railroad Quiz 83

Canals 84

Famous Ship Canals 85

Canal Quiz 85

Answer Keys **86**

Introduction

The history of the United States is an exciting story filled with action and adventure. Students enjoy reading and learning about the heroic and colorful people who built the United States and how the country has changed over the years. While reading about the history of the country can be exciting, in order for students to have a real understanding of how the nation began and how it developed, it is important for them to see and study maps to graphically show how these changes have taken place. Reproducible outline maps that illustrate these changes are vital if students are to really understand the history of the United States. Fortunately, most history books have some maps dealing with various events in history. The problem is that many of these maps do not reproduce well or may not really provide all of the information the teacher feels is important. Probably the biggest problem is that the majority of history books just do not have enough maps that illustrate important historical events.

Most teachers have recognized this problem and over the years have developed a system of locating maps to teach various units. One history book may have a good map of the Oregon Trail while another book has an excellent map of the Northwest Territory. Still another shows the original thirteen colonies. And somewhere in the teacher's filing cabinet is a map illustrating how the United States looked just before the Civil War. The problem is finding them all. After the map is located, the teacher must then present the event being studied in a way that will utilize the specific features of the map they are using. Finally, the teacher must create a meaningful activity that will reinforce the students' understanding of the event.

The purpose of this book is to solve this problem. Maps that illustrate the important historical and political events in the history of the United States are included. The maps are drawn and designed so that they can easily be reproduced for classroom distribution, projected for classroom discussion, or scanned so they can be used in computers for class projects. In addition to each map, a brief explanation of the historical event and a related activity intended to reinforce an understanding of the event are included.

The book chronicles the history of what is now the United States from the time of the Ice Age to the admission of Alaska and Hawaii as the forty-ninth and fiftieth states. There are maps that illustrate the discovery of the continent and its colonization and settlement. There are also maps that detail how the United States became a nation. There are maps of the wars fought in America. And there are maps showing the gradual expansion of this great country that began with settlements and expanded until it reached from the Atlantic Ocean in the East to the Pacific Ocean in the West and from Canada in the North to Mexico in the South. Explanations are given of how the expansion occurred, as well as activities that help students re-member what they have learned.

Only maps of those events that occurred in the continental United States are included. Space did not permit maps that show events, such as wars, that happened outside the borders of the United States.

iv

Ice Age in North America

Everyone knows it is hot in the summer and cold in the winter. We also know that sometimes we have a mild winter or a cool summer. This is usually a rare occurrence, and the following year we return to the normal cycle of a hot summer or a cold winter. Scientists tell us, however, that this has not always been the case. The earth's temperature has fluctuated considerably since the planet was formed. There have been several periods where the temperature remained cold on most parts of the earth year-round. Without warm temperatures to melt the winter snow and ice, great sheets of ice were formed at the poles and began to expand. These sheets are called **glaciers**, and if they do not melt, they become larger and larger, covering more land. Once the ice covers a large area of the earth, that area remains cold all of the time, and the hot summer and cold winter cycle does not occur. An extended cold period with a glacial ice covering is called an **Ice Age**.

There have been several Ice Ages throughout the history of the earth. The most recent Ice Age occurred during the **Pleistocene Period** and is the one that most people refer to when they talk about the Ice Age . This Ice Age began about 2.5 million years ago. The ice began to accumulate at the poles and grow. Eventually, over one-third of the earth was covered in ice. In North America, the ice covered almost all of what is now Alaska, Canada, and several northern states that are part of the United States today. It covered most of the areas that are now Illinois and Indiana and parts of Ohio and Missouri. For most of the Ice Age, humans did not live in North America. Sometime during the Ice Age, prehistoric humans came to North America from Asia.

North America had many strange and interesting animals during the Ice Age. There was the **woolly mammoth**, a **mammal** that looked like a large, hairy elephant. There was also the **mastodon** and the **musk ox**. The mastodon was smaller than the mammoth, but it also resembled an elephant with long, curving **tusks**. There was a **saber-toothed tiger**, a vicious **predator** that used its two large **fangs** to kill its prey. There were also camels, shaggy horses, llamas, yaks, and tapirs. And there were many animals that still exist today, but the prehistoric versions were much larger. Some examples are the giant beaver, the giant sloth, and the giant **armadillo**. By the end of the Ice Age, many creatures had disappeared from North America, and some had even become **extinct**. There were no **dinosaurs** living in the Ice Age. Dinosaurs had become extinct centuries before.

We know these strange animals existed because scientists have found their bones and fossils buried in many places in North America. Many bones of **prehistoric** animals have been found in the **La Brea tar pits** in Los Angeles. Some mammoths have been found frozen in ice in **Siberia**. Further proof of the existence of the these animals has been found in caves. Prehistoric artists drew pictures of these creatures.

About 10,000 years ago, the earth began to warm, and the great sheets of ice that covered a large portion of North America retreated back to the poles. Some scientists said that this was the end of the Ice Age. Other scientists feel that the Ice Age that began 2.5 million years ago is not over. In fact, there are still glaciers in Canada, Alaska, and Europe. There are ice sheets in Glacier National Park in Montana and in Greenland and Antarctica.

Lake Agassiz

When the earth warmed at the end of the Ice Age, many things happened. The great sheets of ice that covered almost one-third of the earth retreated back to the poles. The fertile soil the glacier picked up from the north was deposited in the portion of North America that is now known as the **corn belt**. It also left piles of rocks and gravel called **moraines**. A great deal of the glacier did not retreat northward but actually melted. This resulted in flooding and rising of ocean levels. As the glaciers moved, they changed the appearance of the earth. They picked up boulders and rocks from one location and deposited them somewhere else. They crushed pebbles and rocks, creating soil. They polished bedrock, left sand and gravel piles, and sliced through the earth, creating big valleys. They also gouged both huge and small holes in the earth. As the glaciers melted, these holes filled with water and became lakes. This is how the **Great Lakes** and other lakes were formed.

A huge lake was formed at this time but no longer exists. It is called **Lake Agassiz** after Louis Agassiz, a scientist who studied the Ice Age. It is estimated that Lake Agassiz covered 110,000 square miles in what is now northwestern Minnesota, northern North Dakota, southwestern Ontario, southern Manitoba, and Saskatchewan. In order to judge the immense size of Lake Agassiz, look at a map of the United States and find **Lake Superior**, the largest lake in North America. Lake Superior is only one-third the size of Lake Agassiz.

While Lake Agassiz eventually drained and no longer exits, there are many smaller lakes such as Rainy Lake, Red Lake, Lake of the Woods, Lake Winnipeg, and Lake Winnipegosis where Lake Agassiz was originally formed.

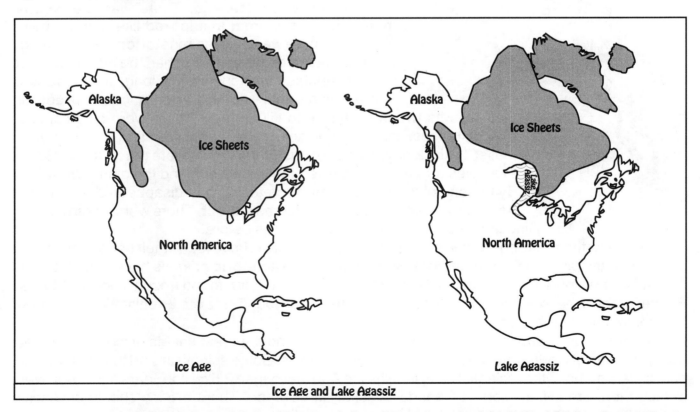

The ice sheets covered what is now Greenland, Canada, and much of the United States. As the sheets began to retreat, Lake Agassiz was formed in Canada and the United States.

2

Name: _____ Date: _____

Ice Age Definitions

Listed at the bottom of the page are a number of terms relating to the Ice Age. Match these terms with the definitions shown below.

1. A creature that survives by killing and eating other creatures. _____

2. A large animal native to northern Canada and Greenland. It has _____ wide, flat, curved horns. It has a shaggy coat and a musky odor.

3. The largest of the Great Lakes. _____

4. An accumulation of tar in what is now Los Angeles. During the Ice _____ Age animals coming to drink became trapped. _____

5. An accumulation of stones, boulders, and debris left by a glacier. _____

6. A huge glacial lake formed in what is now Canada and the northern _____ United States. It no longer exists.

7. A vicious predator that used its two large teeth to kill its prey. _____

8. A prehistoric animal that was similar to an elephant. _____

9. Extended period where the temperature is cold and sheets of ice _____ cover the earth.

10. Masses of snow and ice that move. _____

11. A group of five large lakes in central North America. _____

12. The period of time that began 1.7 million years ago and includes _____ the Ice Age. _____

13. No longer living. _____

14. Giant reptiles that existed during the Mesozoic era. _____

15. A prehistoric animal that was similar to an elephant with long hair _____ and curving tusks.

16. The region where the soil and climate is ideal for raising corn. _____

17. The Asian part of Russia. _____

18. A toothlike projection found on elephants and wild boars. _____

19. Warm-blooded animals that nurse their young. _____

20. A long, pointed tooth. _____

21. Before recorded history. _____

22. A burrowing animal covered with bony plates that act as armor. _____

armadillo, extinct, corn belt, dinosaurs, fang, glaciers, Great Lakes, Ice Age, La Brea tar pits, Lake Agassiz, Lake Superior, mammals, mastodon, moraines, musk ox, predator, Pleistocene Period, prehistoric, saber-toothed tiger, Siberia, tusks, woolly mammoth

Discovering the Americas

If someone were to ask you who discovered America, how would you answer? The Vikings? Norsemen? Eric the Red? Leif Ericson? Columbus? If you guessed any one of these, you would be wrong. Thousands of years before any of these explorers ventured into North America, someone else discovered the continents now known as North and South America. Their descendants were living on these continents centuries before European explorers arrived. Today their descendants are called Native Americans or American Indians. Some people may think that Native Americans have always lived on these continents. This is not true. There was a time when no humans lived in what is now known as the Americas. There were many exotic and interesting animals living on these continents, but no people.

How these people got to the Americas was a puzzle for many years. Scientists now believe that they arrived during the last Ice Age in the Pleistocene Period. During the Ice Age, a great deal of the earth's water had become glaciers. Consequently, there was less water in the oceans than there is today. Some scientists estimate that the oceans may have been more than 300 feet lower during the Ice Age than they are today. The lower oceans made the continents and islands larger. In some cases, the oceans were so low that continents that are separated today were connected then. One example is the two continents Asia and North America. Today, they are separated by the Bering Strait. The Bering Strait is the part of the ocean that separates Siberia from Alaska. It is 55 miles wide, but the water is not very deep. During the Ice Age, though, the lower ocean level revealed a connection, or land bridge, between these two continents. This land bridge is named Beringia. It was named after the Bering Strait. Scientist theorize that sometime during the Ice Age, humans came from Asia to North America in search of food. They walked over this land bridge and eventually populated both North and South America.

Scientists disagree on when humans came to the Americas. Many believe that most emigrated to North America sometime between 40,000 and 13,000 years ago. It is likely that the first Americans did not come all at once, but came in waves, several thousand years apart. Some may have even paddled from Asia around the Aleutian Islands in small canoes made of animal skins.

These prehistoric people, sometimes called the Clovis People, who first came to North America, were hunters and gatherers looking for food. Since they came from Asia, they were of the Mongolian race, the same as Japanese, Chinese, Koreans, and other Asians. Archeologists have discovered that the physical features of Native Americans are similar to people living in Siberia. They have straight black hair, dark eyes, reddish-brown skin, and little hair on their bodies.

When these people came to North America, they found the food plentiful and remained on the continent. They first lived in North America, but some migrated to the south and eventually to what is now South America. These were the people who discovered America. When Columbus arrived, there were millions of descendants of these brave and hardy people already living in what we now call the Americas. They had developed many sophisticated societies such as the Mayan Civilization on the Yucatan Peninsula in Mexico, the Incan Civilization in Peru, and the Aztec Civilization near Mexico City. The various tribes or nations of Native Americans spanned the continents, from coast to coast. They were living as far north as Alaska and Canada and as far south as what is now Chile on the tip of South America.

Name: _____ Date: _____

Route of the First Americans

On the map showing the route of Asians to North America, locate and label the following locations.

1. Bering Strait   2. Pacific Ocean   3. Aleutian Islands   4. Chuckhi Sea
5. Bering Sea   6. Alaska   7. Siberia   8. Yucatan Peninsula
9. Greenland   10. Iceland   11. Newfoundland   12. Beringia

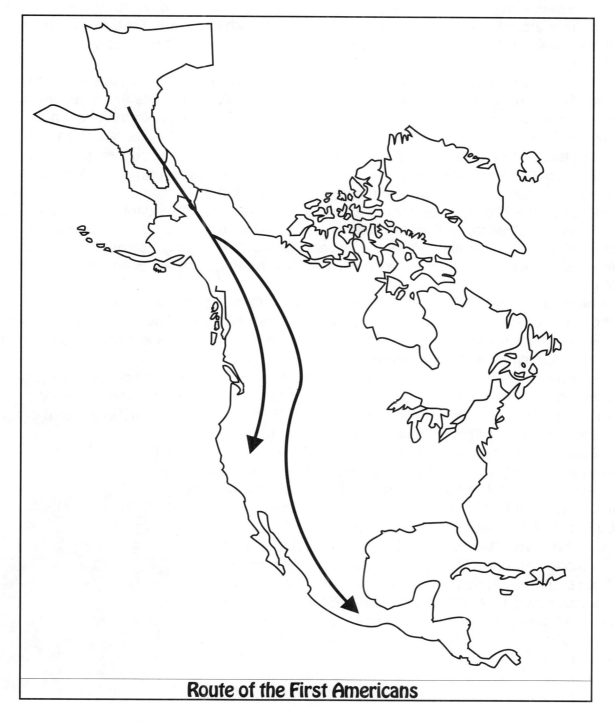

Route of the First Americans

America's Earliest Settlers

The early Americans who crossed the Bering Strait to inhabit what is now North America migrated to the East and to the South. They gradually spread throughout the continent. Some traveled even farther and settled in what is now Central and South America. They adapted to their new environments. Those near the ocean were fishermen. Those who lived where there was a lot of game such as buffalo, were hunters. Others were farmers or foragers. A **forager** is someone who gathers plants and berries. Most combined several of these practices to exist. Over a period of time, the people in each area of the country became distinctive and developed their own cultures different from the others. The tribes within these areas, while not identical, were similar. Listed below and shown on the map are the five main groups of Native Americans before Europeans came to the continent.

Arctic and Subarctic—When humans first crossed from Asia to North America, many settled close to where they crossed and never migrated south as others did. The Arctic culture stretches from southern Alaska to Siberia and around the northern edge of North America to eastern Greenland. The two primary Native American groups found in this region are the Eskimo, also called the Inuit, and the Aleuts of the Aleutian Islands. The Subarctic culture includes all of the Indian tribes of Canada and south to the Great Plains, except those found on the Northwest Coast and the Arctic margin. The Indians that comprise these groups are mainly hunters and fishers.

Northwest—The Northwest corner of the United States was abundant with game and fish for the people who settled there. Caribou, deer, moose, mountain sheep and goats, along with several varieties of roots and berries, provided a rich and varied diet. Fishing, however, provided most of the food. Several kinds of salmon, as well as halibut, herring, whales, clams, and oysters, were plentiful.

Intermountain—Located east of the Northwest Coast to the Rocky Mountains and to the coast of what is now California, were a number of peaceful tribes. They were foragers, which is another word for gatherers. Much of their diet consisted of berries, seeds, roots, fruits, and nuts. They also ate salmon and other game.

Southwest—The Southwest, a hot, arid region, was the homeland of both foraging people and farmers. Many tribes living in this area built houses that were more than one story high. The Anasazi tribe were the ancestors of the present-day Pueblo people and built elaborate homes into cliffs. Some of these cliff dwellings are still standing today.

Plains—The plains extended from the Rocky Mountains to the Mississippi River and from southern Canada to the Gulf of Mexico. The tribes that lived in this area were **nomadic**, which means they moved around a lot. Much of their food and life revolved around the buffalo, which were plentiful in this area.

Eastern Woodlands—The Eastern Woodlands culture, which reached from the Mississippi River to the Atlantic Ocean and from southern Canada to the Gulf of Mexico, covered most of the eastern part of what is now the United States. Tribes in this area lived mainly in villages. The vastness of this region allowed for great differences among the people. Some farmed, others fished or hunted, and others foraged. Many did a little of each. Some were war-like, while others were peaceful.

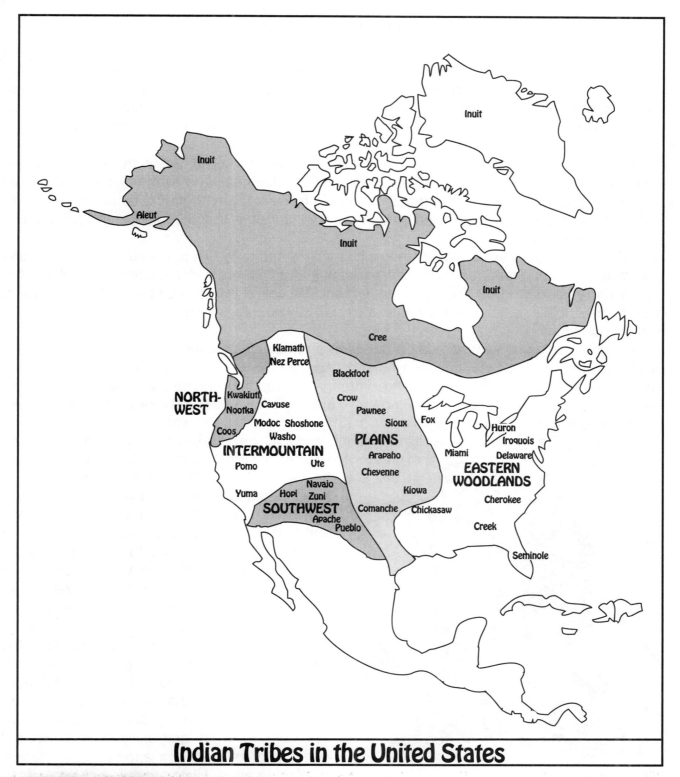

Inuit

Inuit

Aleut

Inuit

Inuit

Cree

Klamath
Nez Perce

Blackfoot

**NORTH-
WEST**

Kwakiutl
Nootka

Cayuse

Crow

Pawnee

Fox

Coos

Modoc Shoshone

Sioux

Washo

PLAINS

Huron
Iroquois

INTERMOUNTAIN

Ute

Arapaho

Miami

Delaware

Pomo

Cheyenne

**EASTERN
WOODLANDS**

Yuma

Hopi

Navajo
Zuni

Kiowa

Cherokee

SOUTHWEST

Apache
Pueblo

Comanche

Chickasaw

Creek

Seminole

Indian Tribes in the United States

Viking Voyagers

Vikings were the first Europeans to land in the New World. They were pirates that originally came from Scandinavia. **Scandinavia** referred to the northern part of Europe and included the area that is today known as Denmark, Norway, and Sweden. Vikings were both feared and fearless. They sailed the oceans looking for food and wealth. They were excellent sailors and used the stars instead of instruments to guide them on their journeys.

About A.D. 870, the Vikings, also known as Norsemen, sailed westward and discovered Iceland, an island west of Norway. They established a settlement, and over the years, those who remained in this settlement prospered and became farmers. They formed a democratic government and developed a beautiful and comprehensive literature that reveals the history of these people and their country.

About 100 years after that first Icelandic settlement, Eric the Red, a Viking leader, decided to sail west. He found land, and although much of it was covered with a glacier, he explored the land for three years and established a settlement. He called the land Greenland to encourage others to move to his settlement. He successfully led 500 people to his new settlement and the land he had discovered.

Eric the Red's son was named Leif Ericson and was sometimes called Leif the Lucky. He heard the story of another Viking, Bjarni Herjulfson, who had made a mistake while sailing to Greenland and passed it, but found another country with beautiful and heavy forests. Many people believe that he had seen what we now know as North America. Leif Ericson decided to go to these forests and get wood to build new ships. In 1001, Leif set sail to the west.

Eventually, Leif arrived in a land that not only had thick forests, but it also had an abundance

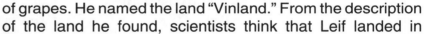

of grapes. He named the land "Vinland." From the description of the land he found, scientists think that Leif landed in Newfoundland, which is now the easternmost province of Canada. He explored this new land and probably traveled southward to Nova Scotia and other parts of the coast that is now known as New England. A settlement was established in this new land, but did not last long. Several other Viking expeditions occurred at later dates.

Since the people of Iceland had little to do with those who lived in southern Europe, the discovery of this new land remained a secret from the rest of the world. In fact, exact information about Viking expeditions is scarce and unreliable even today. The problem is that the Vikings did not write their discoveries down, but rather told them to one another. The stories, called **sagas**, were passed down from generation to generation. Historians did not know if the stories were true or if they were just created in the imaginations of bragging sailors. Several years ago, however, scientists found evidence that there was a Viking settlement in Newfoundland that dated back several centuries. The excavation provides evidence for the Viking sagas that tell of Leif Ericson's voyage and the settlement that he established in the New World.

Viking Voyages Map Activity

Name: _____ Date: _____

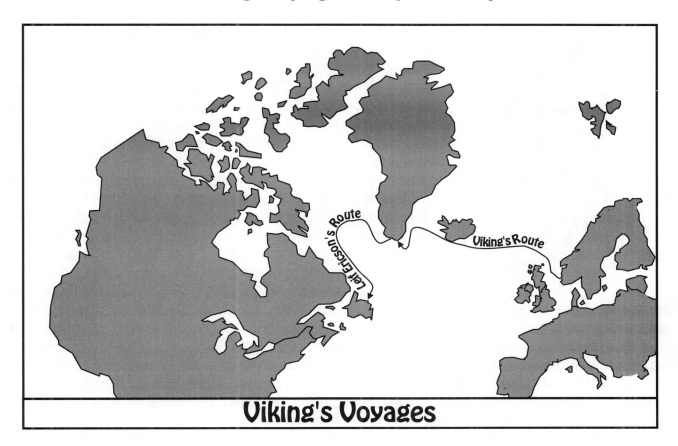

Viking's Voyages

1. Vikings sailed from Scandinavia to explore Iceland, Greenland, and North America. On the map shown above, identify and write in the names of the following.

Atlantic Ocean	**England**	**Europe**	**Greenland**
Iceland	**Newfoundland**	**Nova Scotia**	**North America**
Scandinavia			

2. For many years, people felt that Christopher Columbus was the first European to come to the Americas. There is quite a bit of evidence today that Vikings were here before Columbus. Why do you think the Vikings were not given credit for their explorations sooner?

_____

_____

_____

_____

Christopher Columbus

Asians had crossed the Bering Strait and had been living in what we now call North America thousands of years before Columbus was born. The Vikings had explored and settled in parts of what is now Canada and the United States 500 years before Columbus's first voyage, yet most people give Christopher Columbus credit for discovering the "New World."

Christopher Columbus was an Italian navigator who was born in Genoa in 1451. As a young boy, he went to sea and gained a great deal of sailing experience before he decided to sail to Asia. He had read the famous travel book written by Marco Polo, which told of his exciting adventures in Asia during the thirteenth century, and like many Europeans, Columbus wanted to travel to Asia for spices, silk, gold, and other goods.

But Columbus had a different idea. He wanted to reach the Indies by a new route—the sea. In Columbus's time "the Indies" referred to India, Japan, and China. While most educated people of Columbus's time knew the earth was round, few believed that Asia could be reached by traveling west instead of east. Columbus, however, believed that it was possible to sail west to get to Asia. The fact that no one had ever traveled west to visit Asia did not bother Columbus. What he was mainly concerned about was the distance of the trip. Since no one had ever made the trip before, he did not know how long the voyage would take. He needed to know how much food, water, and other provisions he would need for the journey. He also needed money to finance his trip.

Columbus first asked King John II of Portugal to finance his trip. In return, Columbus promised to bring riches back to Portugal and to claim any new land he discovered for Portugal. The king refused to finance the voyage, so Columbus traveled to Spain to ask King Ferdinand and Queen Isabella for money. He made his request, but the King and Queen were concerned with other state matters and postponed a decision. After seven years, Columbus had given up and was ready to go to France to seek money for his trip, when Queen Isabella agreed to pay for his voyage.

Columbus provided one ship, and Spain provided two other ships. The ships were called the *Pinta*, the *Niña,* and the *Santa Maria.* Columbus and his crew left Palos, Spain, on August 3, 1492, and arrived in the Canary Islands 700 miles away about a week later. After preparing their ships for the voyage, they sailed to the west. They sighted land and went ashore on the morning of October 12, 1492. Most historians believe the land they sighted was an island in the Bahamas. Columbus named this island San Salvador, which means *Holy Savior*. Columbus thought he had reached the Indies, so he called the people he found living there "Indians."

Columbus then sailed to other Islands that are now called the West Indies. He established a settlement on an island he named Hispaniola, which means *Spanish Land.* In January of 1493, he sailed back to Spain where he was praised for finding a new route to the East.

Columbus eventually made three other voyages trying to find India. Instead, he found what is now Puerto Rico, Jamaica, Trinidad, Haiti, Central America, and South America. Since he never brought back treasures or new trade, however, the King and Queen took back the honors they had originally bestowed on Columbus. He died in 1506 disgraced and poor.

Name: _____ Date: _____

Columbus Quiz

Shown below are a number of sentences. Some are true and some are false. If the sentence is true, write the word "true" in front of the sentence. If the sentence is false, write a term that could replace the term written in bold type to make the sentence true.

_____ 1. Columbus's first settlement was named **Hispaniola**.

_____ 2. Columbus was a **Portuguese** navigator.

_____ 3. Columbus's **sisters** were *Niña, Pinta,* and *Santa Maria*.

_____ 4. Columbus wanted to reach the **Indies** by the sea.

_____ 5. Most historians think the land Columbus first saw was in the **Bahamas**.

_____ 6. Columbus thought he had reached the Indies, so he called the people he found living there **Native Americans**.

_____ 7. Columbus eventually made **four** voyages trying to find India.

_____ 8. Columbus wanted to travel to **Venice** for spices, silk, and gold.

_____ 9. The island Columbus first discovered was named **San Salvador**, which means *Holy Savior*.

_____ 10. On October 12, **1942**, Columbus's crew first sighted land.

_____ 11. When Columbus died in 1506, he was disgraced and **rich**.

_____ 12. Columbus read the famous travel book written by **Marco Fydor**.

_____ 13. Columbus asked King Ferdinand and Queen Isabella for **money**.

_____ 14. Most educated people of Columbus's time thought the earth was **flat**.

_____ 15. The Indies referred to **Santa Fe**, Japan, and China.

_____ 16. Columbus first asked King John II of **Italy** to finance his trip.

Columbus made four voyages to the New World. On the first trip, he landed on an island in the Bahama group, which he named San Salvador. On the fourth voyage, which is not shown on the map, Columbus reached what is now Central America.

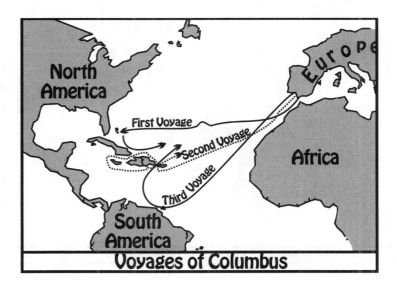

Voyages of Columbus

11

Voyages of Cabot and Vespucci

In 1497, a year before Columbus made his third voyage and saw South America, another sailor from Genoa, Columbus' hometown, sailed to the new world. His name was John Cabot, and he was financed by English merchants who felt that they should compete with Spain and Portugal for newly-discovered lands. Cabot decided to cross the northern Atlantic so that he would not clash with the Spanish or Portuguese claims. It is believed that he was the first European since the Vikings to go ashore in North America. He named the land that he saw "New Found Land." He planted an English flag and claimed the land in the name of King Henry. The next year Cabot again sailed west across the Atlantic. This time he took his son Sebastian with him. Together with a fleet of several ships, Cabot, his son, and the crew explored the coast of North America.

It should be pointed out that while they were exploring the coast of North America, they were still looking for Cathay, which is the ancient name for China. Like Columbus, Cabot's goal was to find a shorter route to the East. In the hold of his ship were goods the English merchants who financed Cabot's voyage hoped to trade. Obviously, he never reached Cathay, and when he returned to England, his sponsors and King Henry were upset that he had failed to trade their goods for the riches in Cathay. They refused to sponsor anymore of his voyages. In spite of their disappointment, England was to later claim all of the land of North America based on Cabot's discoveries.

Although two Italian sailors—Columbus and Cabot—had discovered the new world, it was not named after either one of them. It was named after Amerigo Vespucci, an Italian navigator and geographer who sailed to what is now South America in 1499. Vespucci was the first person to suggest that the lands discovered by Columbus, Cabot, and himself were not really part of Asia but part of a previously unknown continent. A German mapmaker published a description of Vespucci's voyages, along with maps plotting his journey. This mapmaker named the newly-discovered land "America," after Amerigo Vespucci. Originally the name America only referred to Brazil, since this is where Vespucci traveled on two of his voyages. Over time, however, the name referred to all of the western hemisphere.

Cabot 1497
Cabot 1498
North America
Vespucci 1501
Spanish South America

Voyages of Cabot and Vespucci

12

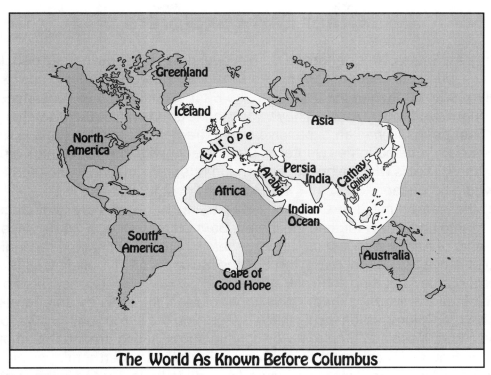

The World As Known Before Columbus

Before Columbus made his famous voyage in 1492, only a small part of the earth had been explored. Vikings had been to Iceland and Greenland. India, Japan, and China had also been visited. Portuguese sailors had sailed down to Africa searching for India. Four years before Columbus made his first voyage, Bartholomeu Dias rounded the southern cape of Africa. The light area indicates the part of the world known before Columbus's voyage.

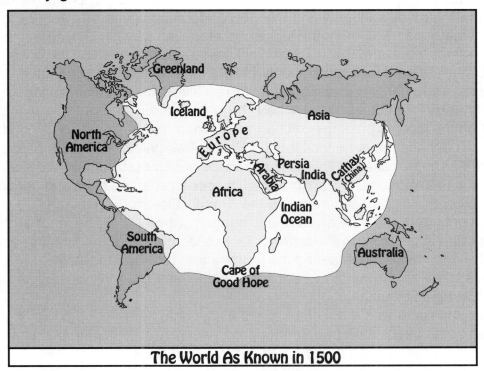

The World As Known in 1500

Just eight years after Columbus made his first voyage, explorers discovered the western shores of the Atlantic and visited what they would eventually learn was two new continents—now named North and South America.

13

Other Early Explorers

Other early explorers of this period did not discover new worlds but helped people understand the world better. During the fifteenth century, Portugal was the world leader in sea exploration, but it was the Italians who controlled the trade with the East. Goods such as silks, dyes, spices, and gems were brought overland by Arabs. They traded these goods with Italian merchants who resold them to other Europeans. It was an expensive way to trade and gave the Italians a monopoly on goods from the East. Other countries wanted to trade directly with the merchants from China, India, and the East Indies. That is why sailors such as Columbus were looking for sea routes to the East. A sea route would be cheaper and safer than traveling over land.

At about the same time that Columbus was trying to get money to finance his voyage westward in order to find a new route to the Indies, Bartholomeu Dias, a Portuguese sailor, sailed to the southern tip of Africa, also looking for new water routes to China and the Indies. He sailed around the tip of Africa but did not reach the East because his crew mutinied. Dias named the tip of Africa, "Stormy Cape," but King John of Portugal changed the name to the "Cape of Good Hope" because he felt that now Portugal had "good hope" of reaching India by an all-water route.

In 1497, before Columbus left on his third voyage, and the same year that Cabot reached the Newfoundland coast, Vasco da Gama, a Portuguese sailor, sailed around the tip of Africa trying to reach India. He followed Dias's route to the Cape of Good Hope, then continued his voyage along the eastern coast of Africa. He eventually located a route to India. By 1513, the Portuguese were regularly trading with China and Japan. Vasco da Gama's voyage was so important that most people forgot all about Columbus. Spurred by Portugal's success, England, France, Spain, and Holland began to send ships around the Cape of Good Hope and also trade with the East.

In spite of the accomplishments of Columbus, Cabot, Vespucci, Dias, and da Gama, no sailor had reached the Indies by sailing west. The person to accomplish this tremendous feat was a Portuguese navigator named Ferdinand Magellan. Magellan was hired by Spain, and in 1519, he set sail with five ships westward toward Brazil. He sailed southward along the coast of what is now known as South America. Magellan not only had to face uncharted seas, unknown dangers in unexplored lands, and a harsh winter, but his own crew also mutinied. The mutiny was crushed and Magellan continued. Eventually, he reached the southern tip of South America and found a passage through the land. A passage or channel of water that joins two larger bodies of water is called a **strait**. This passage is now called the Strait of Magellan. When he passed through the strait, he reached another ocean. This was the same ocean that Balboa had seen seven years before when he was exploring Central America. The ocean seemed calm and peaceful compared to the Atlantic Ocean, so Magellan named it the "Pacific Ocean."

Magellan continued. His crew was sick and hungry, but eventually he reached the Philippines, where he was killed in a fight with the natives. Only one ship out of the five that began, and only 18 sailors of the original 300, completed the journey and returned to Spain.

Magellan's trip was the most extraordinary achievement in the history of navigation and yielded the following information:

- It proved the earth was a sphere and the East could be reached by sailing westward.
- The earth was larger than people thought.
- The Pacific was the largest body of water in the world.
- There was more water on earth than land.
- The lands discovered by Columbus, Cabot, and others were not islands but continents.
- There were no passages south through the new continents. Future explorers would need to explore northward for a passage.

14

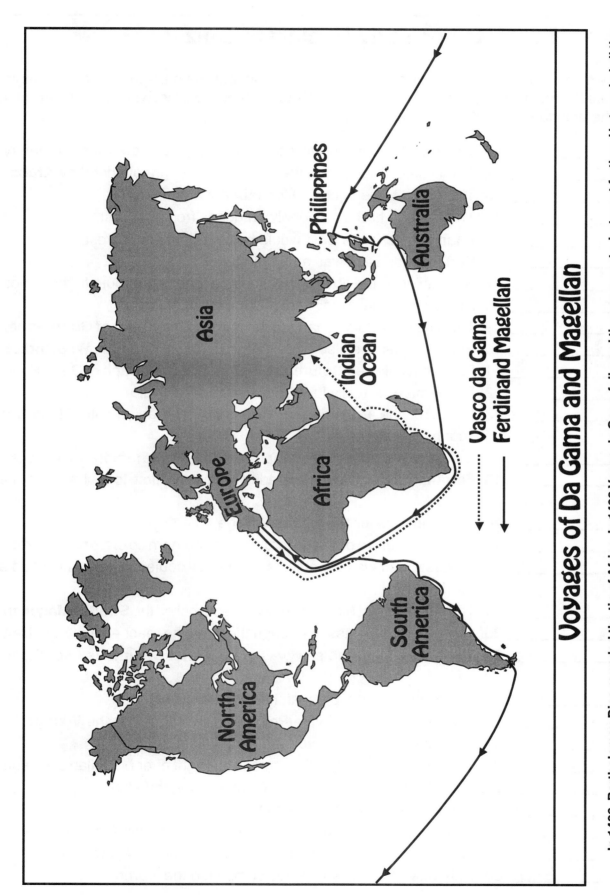

Voyages of Da Gama and Magellan

Vasco da Gama

Ferdinand Magellan

Philippines

Australia

Asia

Indian Ocean

Africa

Europe

North America

South America

In 1486, Bartholomeu Dias rounded the tip of Africa. In 1498 Vasco da Gama followed the same route, but went farther. He traveled all the way to India. Ferdinand Magellan's voyage in 1519 was the first to circle the earth. Magellan was killed by natives in the Philippines, and only one of the original five ships completed the journey.

Name: _____ Date: _____

Other Early Explorers Quiz

Shown below are a number of sentences. Some are true and some are false. If the sentence is true, write the word "true" in front of the sentence. If the sentence is false, write a term that could replace the bold term to make the sentence true.

_____ 1. The **Portuguese** controlled trade with the East in the fifteenth century.

_____ 2. At this time, goods from the East were brought overland by **Arabs**.

_____ 3. The Arabs traded goods with **Italian** merchants.

_____ 4. The **Italians** had a monopoly on goods from the East.

_____ 5. A **land** route to the East would be cheapest and fastest.

_____ 6. Bartholomeu Dias was an **English** sailor.

_____ 7. Dias sailed to the tip of **Africa** looking for a water route to the Indies.

_____ 8. Dias named the tip of Africa, "**Cape Horn.**"

_____ 9. The king of Portugal changed the name to the "**Cape of Good Hope.**"

_____ 10. Vasco da Gama sailed around Africa trying to reach the **West Indies**.

_____ 11. Da Gama followed **Columbus'** route around the Cape of Good Hope.

_____ 12. Da Gama eventually located a sea route to **India**.

_____ 13. By 1513, the **Portuguese** were regularly trading with China and Japan.

_____ 14. Da Gama's voyage was so important that people forgot about **soccer**.

_____ 15. **Ferdinand Magellan's** expedition was the first to sail around the world.

_____ 16. **England** paid for Magellan's voyage.

_____ 17. Magellan found a passage through the southern tip of **North America**.

_____ 18. A passage of water that joins two larger bodies of water is called a **strait**.

_____ 19. The passage that Magellan discovered is called the **Strait of Magellan**.

_____ 20. When Magellan passed through the strait, he reached another **strait**.

_____ 21. The ocean Magellan saw was the one that **Columbus** had discovered.

_____ 22. Magellan named the ocean he saw the "**South Sea.**"

_____ 23. Magellan was killed in the Philippines in a fight with the **Vikings**.

_____ 24. Magellan's voyage proved the earth was a **sphere**.

_____ 25. The earth was **smaller** than people thought after Magellan's voyage.

_____ 26. The **Atlantic** is the largest body of water in the world.

_____ 27. There is **more** water on earth than land.

_____ 28. The lands discovered by Columbus and Cabot were **continents**.

_____ 29. There were **five** passages south through the new continents.

_____ 30. Only **one** of Magellan's ships completed the journey.

16

Spanish Conquistadors

After Columbus made his discoveries known in Europe, several explorers sailing under the Spanish flag came to the New World in search of riches. They were soldiers and were called *conquistadors*, which means "conqueror."

Juan Ponce de Leon. In 1513, a Spanish nobleman named Juan Ponce de Leon heard of a "Fountain of Youth" that was supposed to exist in the new world. He believed that if he found this wonderful fountain and were to bathe in it, he would become young again. He did not find the fountain but instead discovered Florida. He was killed by Native Americans some years later.

Hernando Cortés. Hernando Cortés left Cuba in 1519 and sailed to Mexico. He conquered the Aztec Indians and killed their leader, Montezuma. He robbed the Aztecs of gold, silver, and jewels.

Francisco Pizarro. When the Spanish were conquering Mexico, they heard stories of vast wealth to the south in what is now Peru. Eager to acquire gold, in 1531, Francisco Pizarro assembled about 200 men and set out to find their fortune. After a dangerous journey, they arrived in Peru, overwhelmed the natives, and robbed them of their valuables. He then claimed Peru as part of the Spanish empire.

Francisco de Coronado. In 1540, Coronado set out to find Cibola, the Seven Cities of Gold. It was said that gold and silver in Cibola was so plentiful, that it was used for everyday items, such as tools and utensils. Coronado spent two years looking for this celebrated city. He eventually found it, but it was just a poor Indian town. He returned to Mexico City with only 100 of the original 300 men who began the journey.

Panfilo de Narvaez and Cabeza de Vaca. In 1528, Narvaez mounted an expedition to find riches in the new world, just as Cortés and Pizarro had done. He landed in Florida and explored the southwest. They fought hostile natives, wild animals, and disease, and struggled through jungles. Narvaez was drowned near what is now Galveston, Texas. The survivors continued the exploration. One was named Cabeza de Vaca. After eight years, only four men of the original 300 who began the search were still alive.

Hernando de Soto. Encouraged by the success of Cortés and Pizarro, one of Pizarro's soldiers, Hernando de Soto, decided to make his fortune farther north, in what is now the United States. In 1539, he and his small army landed on the coast of Florida, but he found nothing but jungles, swamps, and poor Indian villages. He continued his journey farther inland and discovered the Mississippi River. He died of fever in 1541, and his men dropped his body into the Mississippi River to hide it from the Indians. Fewer than half of his 600 men returned safely.

Vasco Nuñez de Balboa. In 1513, Vasco Nuñez de Balboa arrived at the Isthmus of Panama as a stowaway. The natives told him of another sea, which he set out to discover. He pushed his party through 45 miles of swamp, forest, and jungles until he found an ocean he called the "South Sea." He claimed the sea in the name of the king of Spain. Seven years later, when Magellan was on his voyage around the world, he also found the same body of water. The ocean was so calm, he named it the "Pacific Ocean."

Name: _____ Date: _____

Spanish Explorers Quiz

Shown below are a number of sentences. Some are true and some are false. If the sentence is true, write the word "true" in front of the sentence. If the sentence is false, write a term that could replace the term written in bold type to make the sentence true.

_____ 1. Cuba is a(n) **peninsula**.

_____ 2. Florida is a(n) **peninsula**.

_____ 3. De Soto spent **three** years exploring along the Mississippi.

_____ 4. St. Augustine was established in **1656.**

_____ 5. **Balboa** sailed from Panama and went to Peru.

_____ 6. **Ponce de Leon** explored Florida.

_____ 7. **Coronado** spent two years exploring what is now the southwestern part of the United States.

_____ 8. **Pizarro** spent four years exploring what is now the southwestern part of the United States.

_____ 9. **De Soto** sailed from Cuba and landed in Veracruz.

_____ 10. **Cortés** marched from Veracruz to Tenochtitlan.

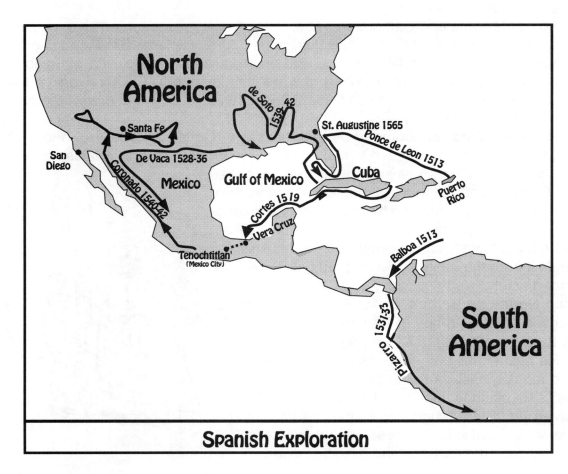

Spanish Exploration

18

Name: _____ Date: _____

Spanish Conquistadors Quiz

Fill in the blank with the correct answer.

1. Ponce de Leon was looking for: _____

2. The first European to see the Pacific Ocean was: _____

3. Spanish explorers were called: _____

4. Cortés conquered the civilization called the: _____

5. Cortés conquered the country we now call: _____

6. The Spanish were mainly interested in finding: _____

7. Pizarro conquered the country we now call: _____

8. Ponce de Leon explored the area that is now the state of: _____

9. The Aztec leader that Cortés killed was: _____

10. What is the name of the country that Pizarro claimed for Spain?_____

11. Where did Narvaez land when he explored the southwest?_____

12. Narvaez was drowned near the city that is now known as: _____

13. One survivor of Narvaez' party was named: _____

14. How many survivors were there of Narvaez' party? _____

15. Coronado set out to find the Seven Cities of: _____

16. These Seven Cities were called: _____

17. Instead of the Seven Cities, Coronado found: _____

18. De Soto discovered a river we now call the: _____

19. When de Soto died, his men dropped his body into the: _____

20. De Soto's men wanted to hide his body from the: _____

21. Balboa discovered an ocean he called the: _____

22. This ocean was later named: _____

23. The explorer who renamed the ocean Balboa discovered was: _____

24. Balboa learned of the sea from the: _____

25. Balboa arrived at the Isthmus of Panama as a: _____

26. *Conquistadors* means: _____

27. How many miles did Balboa travel before he reached the ocean? _____

28. Ponce de Leon was a Spanish: _____

19

French Explorers

At the time Spanish explorers were exploring the southern parts of North America and parts of Central and South America, France also sent explorers to North America. However, their expeditions were sent to the northeast. There were fewer French expeditions, because France was entangled in a number of wars.

Two years after the successful voyage around the world by the crew of Magellan, the king of France decided his country should also become involved in exploring the new world. He sent Giovanni da Verrazano, an Italian sailor, on an expedition to find a northwest passage to the East Indies. In March 1524, Verrazano sighted the coast of what is now North Carolina. He continued north and entered New York Bay and anchored at what is now Newport, Rhode Island. He then sailed to Newfoundland, and when his provisions began to run low, he returned to France.

Since Verrazano had failed to find a northern route to the East, the king sent Jacques Cartier in 1534. While sailing along the east coast of North America, he discovered the St. Lawrence River and explored it. Cartier named the country he had discovered "New France." This voyage gave France a claim to part of North America. The New France Cartier had discovered is now known as Canada.

About 70 years later, in 1608, Samuel de Champlain, a French explorer and fur trader, came to New France and established a fort and built a settlement called Quebec. Champlain explored the Great Lakes as he was searching for a route to China. He also discovered Lake Champlain. The maps Champlain drew, along with his record of events, made this area of the world known to Europe. Champlain lived with the Indians, traded with them, and became their friend.

Two other French explorers, Father Jacques Marquette and Louis Joliet had very different backgrounds. Father Marquette was a French priest sent to America to be a missionary among the Indians. Louis Joliet, born in Quebec, Canada, went to Europe to study, and then returned to Canada to search for copper. He was a trader, a trapper, and a mapmaker. Father Marquette learned from the Indians of a great river that started in the north and flowed south to the sea. This was the Mississippi River that the Spanish explorer Hernando de Soto had discovered. In 1673, Louis Joliet was chosen to explore this river. Father Marquette was picked as the chaplain of the expedition. Marquette and Joliet set out from Lake Michigan, went up the Fox River, traveled over land to the Wisconsin River, and finally made it to the Mississippi. They sailed down the Mississippi as far as Arkansas. They discovered that the Mississippi flowed into the Gulf of Mexico and not the Pacific.

Perhaps the greatest French explorer was Robert de La Salle. La Salle was inspired by Marquette's expedition down the Mississippi. He traveled down the Mississippi River, discovered the Ohio River, and eventually reached the mouth of the Mississippi in 1682. By doing so, he was able to claim the entire Mississippi valley for France. He named this newly-claimed land "Louisiana" in honor of the French King, Louis XIV.

Name: _____ Date: _____

French Explorers Puzzle

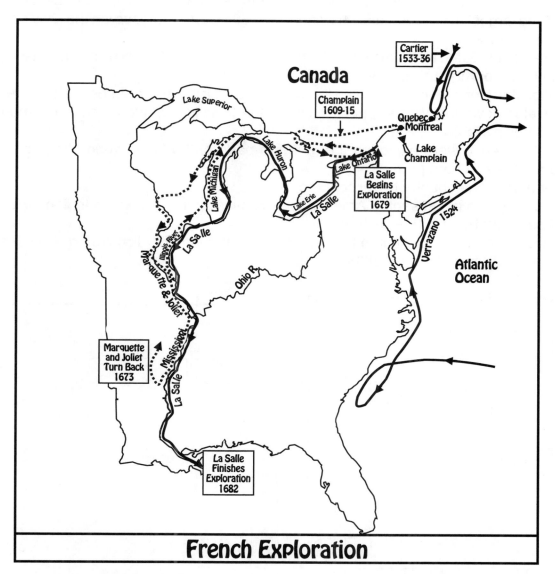

At one time, France owned a great deal of what is the United States today. These vast holdings in North America are based on successful explorations after the continent was discovered. Complete the puzzle on the next page by answering the following questions about French explorers and their discoveries. After you have finished the puzzle, read down the circled letters, and it will reveal the name of one of the most famous French leaders of all time. He was the ruler when the United States bought the Louisiana Territory from France.

1. Although an Italian, he explored for France in 1524.
2. In 1608 this French explorer came to New France and built a settlement called Quebec.
3. Joliet, Marquette, and La Salle all explored this great river.
4. A trader, trapper, and mapmaker, he explored the Mississippi with a partner.
5. Cartier visited an Indian village near a high hill he named Mont Real. In 1642 this Canadian city was founded on the banks of the St. Lawrence River.
6. La Salle sailed through this lake. It is the fourth largest of the Great Lakes.

Name: _____ Date: _____

7. While La Salle was exploring the Mississippi River, he also discovered this river.

8. Just to the north of the United States, this country is the world's second largest country.

9. This is the largest of the Canadian provinces. In 1534 Cartier discovered the area and claimed the land for France.

10. Explored by La Salle, the name given to this land, which included the entire Mississippi valley, was in honor of King Loiuis XIV.

11. La Salle, Marquette, and Joliet sailed through this lake. It is the third-largest of the Great Lakes.

12. He traveled down the Mississippi, discovered the Ohio River, and reached the mouth of the Mississippi in 1682.

13. While the French were exploring the northern parts of the New World, these people were exploring the southern parts.

14. Cartier named the country he discovered "_____ _____ ."

15. He was a French priest sent to America to be a missionary among the Indians. He explored the Mississippi River with a partner.

16. He discovered the St. Lawrence River and named the land he discovered "New France."

17. King Louis XIV was the ruler of this country.

Write the name of the famous French leader: _____

1.

2.

3.

4.

5.

6.

7.

8.

9.

10.

11.

12.

13.

14.

15.

16.

17.

English Explorers

While John Cabot claimed part of North America for England in 1497, the English did not follow up on the claim for many years. About 40 years later, Cartier had claimed for France some of the same land Cabot had claimed. At the end of the sixteenth century, England renewed her interest in the New World. Magellan had succeeded in reaching the Indies by sailing southwest, but the trip was too long . English explorers continued to search for a shorter "northwest passage" to the Indies. From 1576 to 1616, English sailors such as Martin Frobisher, John Davis, Henry Hudson, and William Baffin searched the north for a passage to the Indies. None of these expeditions were successful.

During this same period, Queen Elizabeth I urged some of her sea captains to challenge Spain's land claims and to break the trade monopoly Spain had developed. These English captains built up the English navy so that it was strong enough to challenge Spain's navy. At every opportunity, these English sailors intercepted Spanish ships laden with treasure from the New World and robbed them. Perhaps the most famous English captain at this time was Francis Drake. He plundered Spanish ships as he sailed around the world. The route he followed was similar to the one Magellan had charted about 60 years before. Queen Elizabeth was so impressed with Drake's accomplishments that she knighted him on the deck of his ship when he arrived back in England in 1580.

The Spanish were angry that their ships and ports were being looted by the English. So they built up their navy, and eight years after Drake's trip around the world, they sent their fleet into the English Channel. Their fleet was called the Armada, and they intended to challenge the English navy. The Spanish ships were old, large, and clumsy. The English ships were smaller, lighter, and more easily maneuvered. The Spanish Armada proved no match for the faster, smaller English ships. During the battle, a storm arose, which further hindered the Spanish. The Armada fled, and England began its rise to rule the oceans.

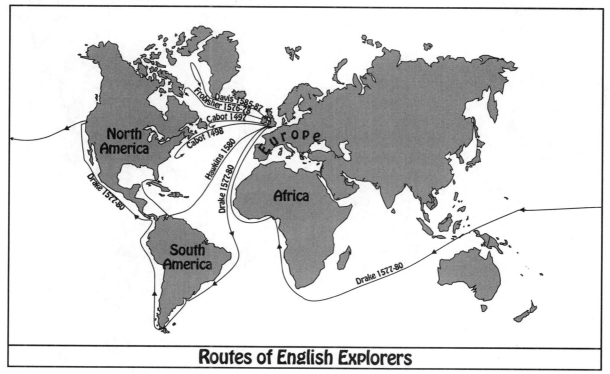

Routes of English Explorers

23

Name: _____ Date: _____

Describing the Geographic Features of the United States

When the European explorers came to North America, they found a rich and diverse landscape. Using an atlas, locate each of the major landforms and bodies of water in the United States listed below, and label them on the map.

MOUNTAINS
Rocky Mountains
Appalachian Mountains
Sierra Nevada Mountains
Pacific Coast Ranges

OCEANS AND GULFS
Atlantic Ocean
Pacific Ocean
Gulf of Mexico

RIVERS
Mississippi River
Ohio River
Missouri River
Hudson River
Arkansas River
Colorado River

LAKES
Great Salt Lake
Lake Michigan
Lake Superior
Lake Huron
Lake Erie
Lake Ontario

LAND REGIONS
Mojave Desert
Great Plains

Name: _____ Date: _____

Famous Explorers

Based on the accomplishment shown on the right of the chart, fill-in the appropriate explorer, country, date, and purpose of the voyage. In the column "country," be sure you list the country sponsoring the voyage, not the home country of the captain. Use the explorers listed at the bottom of the page.

Explorer	Country	Date	Purpose	Accomplishment
				Sailed to the southern tip of Africa
				Reached America by sailing west from Europe
				Laid the basis for British claim to North America
				First European to reach India by the sea route
				The explorer after whom the New World was named
				Discovered the Pacific Ocean
				First to circumnavigate the globe
				Conqueror of the Aztecs and Mexico
				Laid basis for French claims in North America
				Conquered Peru
				Discovered and explored the St. Lawrence River
				Discovered the Mississippi River
				Explored the southwestern part of the United States
				Founded Quebec; called the Father of New France
				Explored the Hudson River
				Discovered the Ohio River; explored the Mississippi

Use these names:

Balboa	Cabot	Cartier	Champlain	Columbus	Coronado	Cortés	Da Gama
De Soto	Dias	Hudson	La Salle	Magellan	Pizarro	Verrazano	Vespucci

     25

Name: _____ Date: _____

Who Gets the New World?

Once it was established that Columbus and the explorers who followed were not traveling to the Indies, but were discovering new lands, the question arose, "To whom did the new lands belong?" The question was raised when Cabral, a Portuguese captain, was driven by a storm to the coast of South America. Portugal and Spain claimed the area. The dispute was solved by the Pope in 1493, who was very powerful at the time. He suggested that a line or a meridian be drawn around the world 100 leagues west of the Cape Verde Islands. All of the lands to the east of the line would be given to Portugal, and all of the lands to the west of line would be given to Spain. A year later, Portugual and Spain agreed to move the line 370 leagues west of the Cape Verde Islands.

At the time the line was drawn, no one knew how much land was in the New World. But the division gave the area that is now known as Brazil to Portugal. This is why Portugal settled Brazil. In fact, people still speak Portuguese in Brazil. The rest of South America and all of North America was given to Spain, and King Ferdinand and Queen Isabella began to establish settlements in the West Indies.

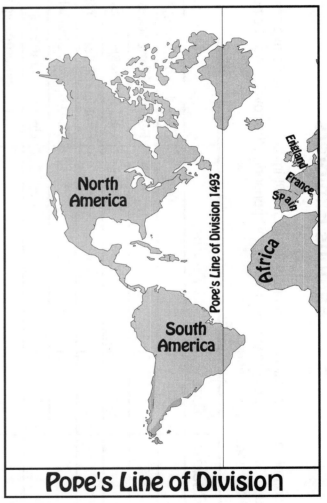

Pope's Line of Division

1. Which country benefited the most from the Pope's decision?

_____

Why? _____

_____

_____

_____

_____

2. What evidence is there today of the Pope's decision?

_____

_____

_____

26

Settlements in the New World

The explorers who discovered the New World had many reasons for their voyages. Some came looking for trade routes. Others wanted adventure or fame. Many were looking for riches—gold, silver, and gems. After a time, most explorers became discouraged when they realized that their voyages would not achieve what they had intended. The explorers did not discover a shorter route to the East. Many died on the voyage or did not reap any benefits from the voyage. While some conquistadors, such as Cortés and Pizarro, did find gold, silver, and jewels and plundered the wealth of the natives, most did not. However, as the explorers came ashore and explored the New World, they found a land that was rich in game, natural resources, and fertile soil. It was the kind of country that would be ideal for establishing colonies. And after awhile, that is exactly what they did. The settlements in the New World varied widely, depending on which country settled in the region, but gradually, the English Colonies dominated the New World.

New Spain

While Columbus and other explorers arrived in the New World in their search for a better route to India and China, many Spaniards had other reasons for their voyages.

- Searching for gold, silver, and other valuables.
- Converting the natives to their Christianity and specifically to Catholicism.
- Creating empires for some Spanish noblemen.
- Profiting from trade.

The very reasons Spaniards explored the New World were the same reasons they decided to establish colonies. In fact, Spanish explorers were the first to establish colonies in the New World. For the most part, Spain colonized the areas that are south of what is now the United States. This new country was called *New Spain,* and Mexico City was at its center. The exploration and colonization spread in all directions from Mexico City. While the first Spanish settlement in the New World was established by Columbus on the island of Hispaniola, which is now Haiti and the Dominican Republic, the first permanent colony on the mainland of what is now the United States was established by a Spanish soldier in 1565. The name of that colony was St. Augustine, and it was located in Florida. St. Augustine is still a thriving city today, and visitors are able to view the remnants of the Spanish settlement established centuries ago.

Most of the Spanish colonists were farmers. Others were engaged in mining gold, silver, and gems. Others mined nonprecious metals such as tin, iron, lead, and copper. Still others raised livestock and harvested lumber. All of these occupations required a great deal of manpower, since there were few machines to do work during this period. The Spanish colonists solved this problem by using the natives and African slaves to work their plantations, mines, and businesses.

When a Spaniard received land in the New Country, the natives who lived on this land were considered part of the land. The landowner could use the natives' labor to create wealth for himself. In effect, the natives were like serfs in Europe—they were bound to the land and controlled by the owner. The natives were often mistreated and overworked by the landowners. Except for some Catholic missionaries, who tried to convert the natives to Christianity, Spanish colonists were cruel to Native Americans.

Name: _____ Date: _____

New Spain Quiz

Shown below are a number of sentences. Some are true and some are false. If the sentence is true, write the word "true" in front of the sentence. If the sentence is false, write a term that could replace the term written in bold type to make the sentence true.

_____ 1. Spain colonized the areas that are **north** of what is now the United States.

_____ 2. Spanish colonists were **nice** to Native Americans.

_____ 3. The first permanent colony in North America still in existence is **Miami**, located in Florida.

_____ 4. Most of the Spanish colonists were **fishermen**.

_____ 5. St. Augustine was established in **1565**.

_____ 6. Spanish colonists used natives and African **farmers** to work their land.

_____ 7. Many Spaniards came searching for **gold**, silver, and other valuables.

_____ 8. Some Spaniards came to convert the natives to **Protestantism**.

_____ 9. When a **Spaniard** received land in the New Country, the natives who lived on this land were considered part of the land.

_____ 10. Spanish explorers found a land that was **rich** in game, natural resources, and fertile soil.

New France and New Netherlands

While the Spanish settled mainly in the south of the New World, the French settled in the north. The French originally came to the New World to find the northwest passage to the East. Later, they came to develop the fur trade. Furs were a thriving business in Europe. Coats, hats, and other clothing were made of animal furs. The abundance of wild animals in North America made fur trading a profitable business.

Samuel de Champlain was the founder of New France. In 1608, Champlain came to New France and established a fort and built a settlement called Quebec. He explored the Great Lakes and discovered Lake Champlain as he was searching for a route to China. Champlain lived with the Indians, traded with them, and became their friend. In contrast to the Spanish, France's contact with Indians was generally friendly. They traded with them and trapped animals together. Rather than forcing the natives to accept their way of life, the French learned to speak native languages and learned how the natives were able to survive in the wilderness.

As the French explored North America, they were not as interested in colonizing immediately as the Spanish were. They claimed great tracts of land in the name of France for future use by Frenchmen. They built forts along the St. Lawrence, the Great Lakes, the Mississippi, and the Ohio. These forts were busy places where trade was carried on and where the priests held Mass. France claimed Nova Scotia, Canada, and the area of the Mississippi River from Canada to Louisiana.

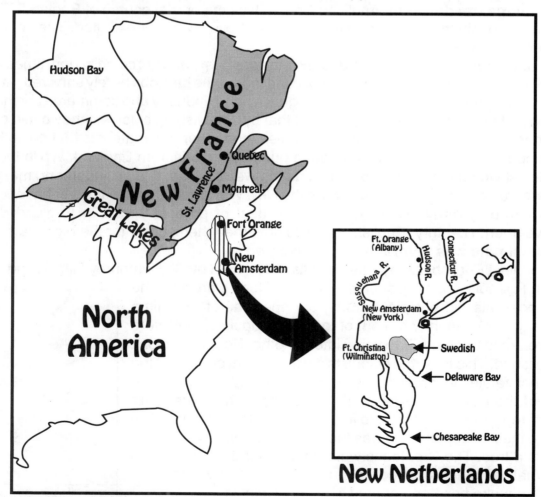

In 1609, Henry Hudson, representing Holland, arrived at what later came to be known as the Hudson River. While Dutch explorers came to the New World to find the northwest passage, settlers from the Netherlands came to develop a fur trade with the Iroquois Indians. The Dutch were not interested in developing real colonies. Their interest was in trade, so they built forts and trading stations. Dutch traders built a settlement called Fort Orange in a place that we now know as Albany, New York. Fort Orange was a thriving fur-trading center and firmly established the Dutch in the New World. In 1623, a settlement was established at the mouth of the Hudson River. This is the spot where New York City is today.

The Dutch colony was called New Netherland. It included not only Fort Orange, but many other settlements along the Hudson, Delaware, and Connecticut Rivers. The colony was expanded in 1626 when the Dutch governor purchased the island of Manhattan from the Indians for trinkets that were said to be worth about $24. The center of New Netherland was called New Amsterdam on Manhattan Island. In 1655, the Dutch took over Swedish settlements along the Delaware River.

New England

The New England colonies in the New World grew more rapidly than those of Spain, France, or the Dutch. While there were many reasons to come to the New World, some of the more common reasons are listed below.

- **Religious freedom**. The Anglican Church was the official church of England. Those who refused to join the church or differed with its beliefs were persecuted. The colonies were opened up to all religions.
- **Opportunities to make a living**. During the greatest period of colonization, times were hard in England. There were not many jobs, and those who had jobs barely survived. At the same time, there were Englishmen who had grown rich in industry and commerce and had money to invest in the colonies. They thought that by establishing colonies, they could grow even richer. They could obtain furs, lumber, fish, and other raw materials that could be sold in Europe. Colonists would also need to purchase goods from England. While the ordinary colonist would not prosper as much as the wealthy from this arrangement, many thought there would be more opportunities in the New World than they would ever have in England.
- **To avoid tyranny**. There was a great deal of political unrest in England during the seventeenth century. English colonists governed themselves for the most part.
- **The climate was favorable to Englishmen**.

The earliest English colony was established in 1585 by Sir Humphrey Gilbert and Sir Walter Raleigh on Roanoke Island, just off the coast of North Carolina. The Roanoke colonists did not plant crops, but spent all of their time looking for gold. When they ran out of food and supplies, they were forced to return to England. Two years later, another Roanoke colony was established. This time, the colonists did try to plant crops, but the soil was not fertile. In order to get more food and supplies, the governor of the colony returned to England. When he returned to Roanoke three years later, he could find no trace of the colonists. The only clue to their disappearance was the word "Croatoan," which was carved into a tree. The Croatoans were a tribe of Indians who lived nearby. What happened to the colonists remains a mystery today. The colony at Roanoke has been named The Lost Colony.

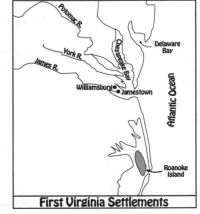

First Virginia Settlements

30

Later English Colonies

While the early attempts by the English to colonize the New Country failed, they did not give up. In the early part of the seventeenth century, many English merchants thought that colonies could provide them with additional markets for their goods. Not only would the colonists need to purchase goods from English merchants, the colonies could produce goods for the merchants that could be sold throughout the world. There was an additional benefit. The New World was rich in furs and natural resources that the rest of the world was willing to pay for. So merchants banded together to form **stock companies** to establish colonies in the New World.

London and Plymouth Companies

Merchants decided that stock companies were a safer way to invest in the colonies, since the earlier English colonies had failed. They reasoned that if many people invested a little money, no one would be risking their entire fortune if the venture failed. Two of the companies that were formed were the London Company and the Plymouth Company. These companies sold shares of their company. Anyone who bought a share would receive a share of any profits made by the company.

Each company received a charter from the king. The London Company was given a strip one hundred miles wide along the seacoast between the mouth of the Potomac and the southern boundary of the present North Carolina. The Plymouth Company was given a similar strip between Halifax in Nova Scotia and Manhattan Island. The middle strip between these two was open to both companies to settle. Part of the area granted in the charter was actually claimed by France. The king, however, believed that Cabot's discovery gave England the right to the entire North American continent.

The charters issued to these two English colonies established certain rules for the government of the colonies. Each company had a council of settlers who regulated trade with the Indians and enforced the laws. The only religion that was permitted was the Church of England. Probably the most important feature of the English colonies was that the settlers were given all of the rights and privileges of English citizens.

Early American Settlements

31

This was unusual because colonies established by other countries did not give colonists the same rights as those living in the mother country. Consequently, settlers from all over Europe chose to settle in the English Colonies.

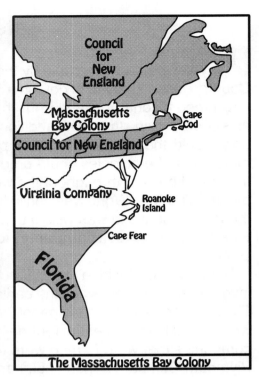

The London Company established the first permanent English settlement in 1607. The name of the new settlement was Jamestown in what is now Virginia. Jamestown was settled on a peninsula on the James River. This location was chosen so the settlers could protect themsleves from attacks from Indians and the Spanish. However, the location turned out to not be as safe as the settlers thought. It was close to marshes that had mosquitoes that carried malaria.

From a business point of view, the London Company never did well. The colonists had little food, some were sick from malaria, and many spent their time looking for gold. At one time, the colony had only seven laborers and 52 colonists who were described as "gentlemen." The gentlemen would do no work but would instead look for gold. If it were not for Captain John Smith, the colony might have failed. But Jamestown did not fail. It grew, and other Englishmen were encouraged to face the risks of the New World.

The Massachusetts Bay Colony

One of the groups of colonists that came after Jamestown were the Pilgrims, who landed in Massachusetts in 1620. The Pilgrims were Protestants who refused to join the Anglican Church, which was recognized as England's church. They originally went to Holland, where they could worship as they wished, but they wanted their children to grow up English. So they set sail on the *Mayflower* and landed at Plymouth Rock.

Other English settlements were established along the coast during this period. At the same time England was establishing colonies, so were other countries.

The Massachusetts Bay Colony

The most successful of the colonies was the Massachusetts Bay Colony. In 1620, a group received a land grant from the English king to establish the colony. The grant stated that the boundaries of their land were between 48° and 40° north latitude and extended westward indefinitely. The people who settled this colony were called Puritans. They left England because they were not permitted to worship as they wanted to in England. Puritans wanted to remain in the Church of England, but they wanted to purify it. That is why they were called Puritans. Strangely enough, while the Puritans came to America for religious freedom, they did not want that same freedom for others. Quakers and those of faiths other than the one the Puritan's practiced were not allowed to stay in the colony. Some were put in prison, while others were driven out, and a few were even hanged. Sometimes those who did not belong to the Puritan's church could live in the colony, but they were not allowed to participate in the government. The right to vote was only given to church members. The Massachusetts Bay Colony became so successful, that over a 10-year period, over 20,000 settlers left England to live there.

Name: _____ Date: _____

Countries That Colonized

Several countries explored the New World, but four countries established extensive colonies. They were the Spanish, French, Dutch, and English. Listed below are statements that relate to the colonies in one of the four countries. Before each statement are the letters "S," which represents Spanish, "F," which represents French, "D," which represents Dutch, and "E," which represents English. Circle the letter to which the statement pertains.

S F D E   1. Originally they came to the New World to find the northwest passage to the East, but later they came to develop the fur trade.

S F D E   2. Colonized the areas that are south of what is now the United States

S F D E   3. Their interest was trade, so they built forts and trading stations.

S F D E   4. Many colonists from this country came to the New World for religious freedom.

S F D E   5. Were the first to establish colonies in the New World

S F D E   6. Many colonists from this country came to the New World to avoid tyranny.

S F D E   7. This country established the first permanent colony on the mainland of what is now the United States in 1565.

S F D E   8. Colonists from this country settled mainly in the north.

S F D E   9. Established a colony in 1585 on Roanoke Island

S F D E   10. One reason this country explored the New World was to search for gold, silver, and other valuables.

S F D E   11. For the most part, these colonists governed themselves.

S F D E   12. The country that established a fort and built a settlement called Quebec

S F D E   13. Many colonists from this country came to the New World just to make a living.

S F D E   14. Columbus established the first settlement on the island of Hispaniola in the name of this country.

S F D E   15. One of this country's colonies is known as The Lost Colony.

S F D E   16. When a person from this country received land in the New World, the natives who lived on the land were considered part of the land.

S F D E   17. These colonies in the New World grew more rapidly than those of other countries.

S F D E   18. These colonists learned to speak native languages.

S F D E   19. One reason this country explored the New World was to convert the natives to their Christianity, specifically to Catholicism.

S F D E   20. Bought the island of Manhattan from the Indians for trinkets that were said to be worth about $24

Name: _____ Date: _____

S F D E   21. Named their colony *New Netherland*

S F D E   22. Mexico City was at the center of this country's colonies.

S F D E   23. What attracted colonists from this country was that the colonies were opened up to all religions.

S F D E   24. Colonists from this country traded and trapped animals with the Indians.

S F D E   25. Built a settlement called Fort Orange in a place that we now know as Albany, New York

S F D E   26. Colonists from this settlement did not plant crops, but spent all of their time looking for gold. They returned to their country when they ran out of food.

S F D E   27. One reason this country explored the New World was to create empires for noblemen.

S F D E   28. Some believe the Croatoan Indians were in some way involved in the disappearance of colonists from this country.

S F D E   29. This country established a settlement that today is known as St. Augustine in Florida.

S F D E   30. Explorers from this country were not interested in colonizing immediately but claimed great tracts of land in the name of their country.

S F D E   31. Established a settlement that is now known as New York City

S F D E   32. Built forts along the St. Lawrence, the Great Lakes, the Mississippi, and the Ohio

S F D E   33. Took over Swedish settlements along the Delaware River

S F D E   34. Established many settlements along the Hudson, Delaware, and Connecticut Rivers

S F D E   35. Claimed the area of Nova Scotia, Canada, and the area of the Mississippi River from Canada to Louisiana

The English Colonies Grow

The small English settlements that began along the coast thrived and eventually grew into 13 colonies. These colonies are generally divided into sections. They are the English colonies, the Middle Colonies, and the Southern Colonies. The English Colonies consisted of Massachusetts, New Hampshire, Connecticut, and Rhode Island. The Middle Colonies consisted of New York, Pennsylvania, New Jersey, and Delaware. The Southern Colonies consisted of Maryland, Virginia, North Carolina, South Carolina, and Georgia.

The way of life was different in each of these groups of colonies. This happened for two reasons. First, the people who settled in each area were different. Those that settled in the New England Colonies were Puritans. They came in the seventeenth century for religious freedom. New England colonists were very religious. On the other hand, the middle colonies were settled by people from many European countries. There were German, French, Irish, Scots, Dutch, and Swedes. They were interested in making money and farming. The first people who came to the Southern Colonies were not primarily interested in religion. They were looking for gold and wanted to get rich quickly by trading with the Indians.

The second difference among the three sections of the 13 colonies deals with geographical conditions. New England has less level land than the other sections. The winters are long and harsh. The ground is rocky. So while the people in New England were able to grow most of their own food, they were unable to grow crops to sell. Consequently, New Englanders earned money by fishing, selling lumber, and trading. The Middle Colonies were able to grow vegetables, fruits, and grain. They grew a lot of corn and wheat and built mills to grind the grain into flour. Because the middle colonies grew so many grains, they were called the "Bread Colonies." They shipped some of their goods overseas. Southern Colonists planted tobacco and rice. The climate and soil made the land good for farms. While there were many small farms, the Southern Colonies were known for their large plantations where a few rich people owned most of the land and used slaves for work. Plantations grew almost all of their food. The typical plantation had 50–100 slaves, although some of the larger plantations had many more.

Name: _____ Date: _____

Knowing the Original Colonies

How well do you know the original 13 colonies? Look at the map below. Identify each colony and write its name in the appropriate space below the map.

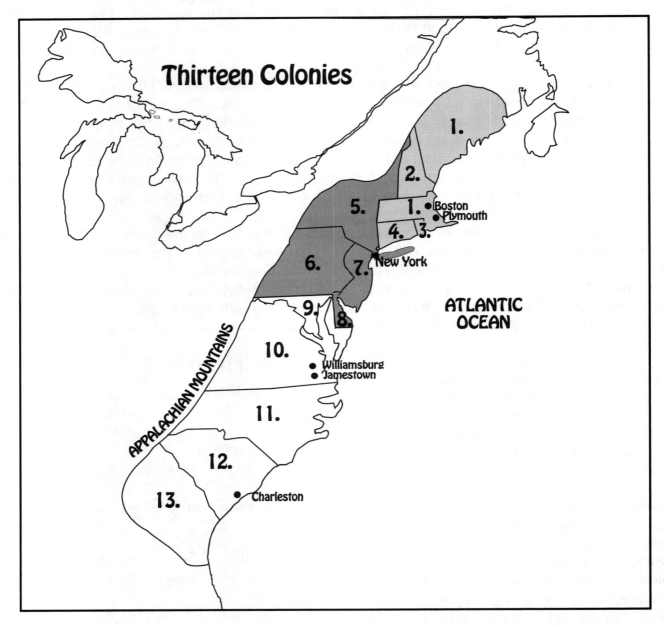

Thirteen Colonies

1.

2.

5.   1. ● Boston
              ● Plymouth

4.   3.

6.   7. ● New York

ATLANTIC
OCEAN

9.   8.

10.

● Williamsburg
● Jamestown

11.

12.

13.   ● Charleston

APPALACHIAN MOUNTAINS

NEW ENGLAND	MIDDLE COLONIES	SOUTHERN COLONIES
1._____	5._____	9._____
2._____	6._____	10._____
3._____	7._____	11._____
4._____	8._____	12._____
		13._____

The French and Indian War

By the eighteenth century, France and England were the strongest nations in Europe and were competing for colonies in many parts of the world. Each wanted to expand and control trade for their country, especially in America. The fur trade in America was very profitable for the French who not only had access to a vast array of wild animals, but could also trade with Native Americans for furs that could also be sold in Europe. England wanted to participate in the fur trade, but they also wanted to expand their colonies and develop farms to the west. There was one problem. The area west of the Appalachian Mountains, which was the most likely place for the English colonists to locate their farms, was claimed by both England and France. It was inevitable that these two world powers would clash over this issue. The conflict between the two powers in North America was just part of the struggle. The conflict was part of a larger war in Europe and on the sea.

The stage was set for a clash between these two countries. In America, the conflict came to be known as the French and Indian War. The name of the war is confusing. Who was fighting? Was it a war between the French and the Indians? Were the British involved? Anyone else? Actually, the French and Indian War was part of a series of armed conflicts between 1689 and 1763, with the English on one side and the French, Austrians, and Spanish on the other. Both sides received help from different groups of Indians.

There were really three wars between England and France over a 50-year period, without either side winning decisive victories. These wars led up to the French and Indian War, which was fought between 1754 and 1763. The three earlier wars were:

- *King William's War*, named for the Dutch king, William, was fought between 1689 and 1697.
- *Queen Anne's War*, named for the English Queen Anne, was fought between 1702 and 1713. This war caused France to lose Newfoundland, Nova Scotia, and the Hudson Bay territories to Britain.
- *King George's War* was fought from 1744 to 1748.

The final war in this series was called the French and Indian War. Both France and Britain claimed the land in the Ohio territory. The French built forts along the rivers in this territory. In 1753, the governor of Virginia sent a young soldier, George Washington, to get the French to leave. They refused. Washington and his men built a fort south of Fort Duquesne [pronounced Doo-kān'] and called it Fort Necessity. The war began in 1754.

Early in the war the French were successful. George Washington was forced to surrender Fort Necessity, and when British general Edward Braddock attempted to attack the French-held Fort Duquesne, he was mortally wounded. In 1758, William Pitt, the British prime minister, began directing the war effort. In 1759, the British attacked Quebec, and after a five-day battle, captured the city. The British captured Montreal in 1760. The British had won. In February 1763, the Treaty of Paris was signed, officially ending the war. The treaty gave Britain title to all French territory east of the Mississippi, including Canada. Britain also gained Florida from Spain, who was France's ally in the war. Spain was given France's territory between the Mississippi River and the Rocky Mountains. France was given a few islands in the Caribbean.

One final note: You may have noticed that at the beginning of the above story, the term "English" is used, and at the end, "British" is used. This is because until 1707 there was no Great Britain. Then the Acts of Union passed by the parliaments of England, Wales, and Scotland united these countries, and they became known as Great Britain.

Name: _____ Date: _____

Map of the French and Indian War

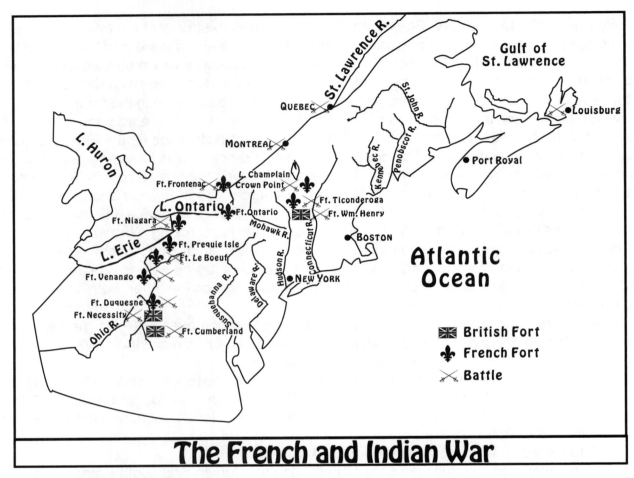

The French and Indian War

Using the map above, make a check in the appropriate boxes.

NAME	BRITISH FORT	FRENCH FORT	NEITHER	BATTLE
1. Niagara				
2. Duquesne				
3. Necessity				
4. Cumberland				
5. Le Boeuf				
6. Prequie Isle				
7. Ontario				
8. Venango				
9. Frontenac				
10. Crown Point				
11. Ticonderoga				
12. William Henry				
13. Port Royal				
14. Louisburg				
15. Quebec				
16. Montreal				

Name: _____   Date: _____

How Well Do You Know Canada?

The Treaty of Paris gave Britain title to all of the French territory east of the Mississippi, including Canada. How well do you know Canada? Most U.S. citizens know very little about our neighbors to the north. Shown below is a map of Canada today. Identify the provinces, and their capitals, and write them on the map. Also, locate and identify the nation's capital.

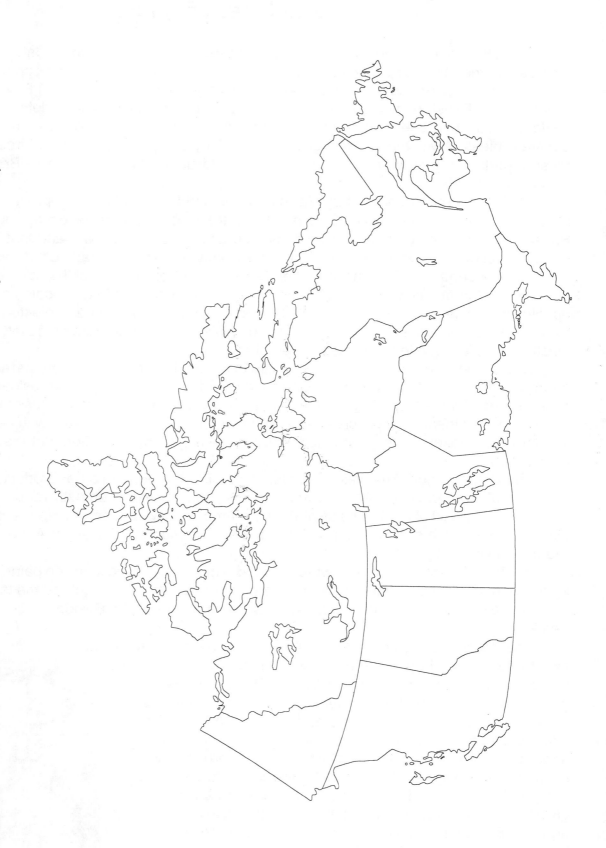

War of Independence

In 1763, Britain had won a tremendous victory over France. By adding Canada and all of the land east of the Mississippi to its empire, Britain controlled more land and people than ever. For the most part, the American colonists were pleased to be part of the British Empire. They were proud of their British origins and pleased with the part they had played in defeating the French. Certainly there had been minor disputes between Britain and the colonies, but colonists were generally pleased with their form of government. They enjoyed a great deal of freedom. Perhaps most importantly, they were prospering. They sold grain, flour, and rice to Britain and other European countries.

While the French and Indian War had increased Britain's land, people, and power, it did produce some negative results. Britain felt that the colonies were becoming too independent. British officials felt that the colonies did not help enough during the war and that Britain needed more control over the colonies. Also, Britain had many debts due, in part, to the wars fought in the colonies. Consequently, Britain took several steps to control the trade of the colonies so that more of the wealth came back to Britain. Britain also wanted to be sure that the colonies did not break up. However, when Britain began her policy toward the colonies, she neglected one important aspect. The British did not consult with the colonists. The change from being left alone to being strictly controlled was too much too fast for the colonists.

One change that was particularly distasteful to colonists were **writs of assistance**. A writ was an official document that gave a British official the right to enter a private residence or storage facility to search for smuggled goods. This regulation, coupled with others, caused upheaval in the colonies. While these new policies were infuriating, the British did not stop with new regulations. They imposed taxes for the first time in the history of the colonies. Some of the new taxes are discussed below.

The Sugar Act of 1764 was a tax placed on sugar, wine, and other products shipped from countries other than Great Britain to the colonies. This tax was eventually reduced.

The Stamp Act placed taxes on all legal documents, newspapers, almanacs, pamphlets, and almost all paper items. The Stamp Act was resisted as much as the Sugar Act was. In 1766, the Stamp Act was repealed.

In 1767 the Townshend Acts were enacted. These acts levied taxes on paint, tea, glass, and lead imported into the colonies. Colonists stopped buying these products so the taxes on imports were repealed, except for the tax on tea. This eventually led to the Boston Tea Party.

The British imposed more restrictions, the colonists resisted, and eventually the war began. When the war started, it was not for the purpose of independence. General George Washington, who would eventually become the first president of the United States, said, "When I first took command of the army, I abhorred the idea of independence." What he was hoping for was "a lasting and happy union with Great Britain." In fact, it is estimated that when the war began, only about 20 percent of the colonists preferred independence. They did not want to lose their ties with England, but at the same time, they felt they should have the same rights as Englishmen. It was not until a year after the war had begun that the Declaration of Independence was adopted.

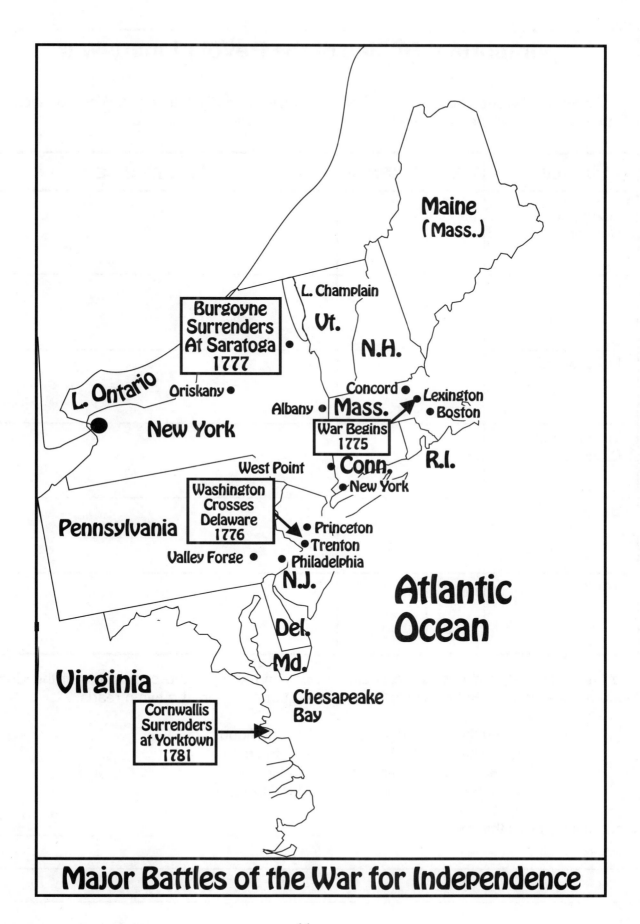

Major Battles of the War for Independence

Name: _____ Date: _____

Important Battles of the Revolutionary War

Shown on the chart below are a number of battles in the Revolutionary War. For each battle, fill in the year, the winner, and the importance of the battle.

BATTLE	YEAR	WINNER	IMPORTANCE
Lexington and Concord			
Bunker Hill			
Long Island			
Trenton and Princeton			
Saratoga			
Yorktown			

The first battle listed above is the subject of a hymn sung at the completion of the Concord Monument, written by Ralph Waldo Emerson. A quotation from the hymn reads:

> By the rude bridge that arched the flood,
>   Their flag to April's breeze unfurl'd,
> Here once the embattled farmers stood,
>   And fired the shot heard round the world.

What exactly does this mean? _____

_____

_____

Name: _____ Date: _____

Patriots of the American Revolution

Listed below are descriptions of American patriots. Write the name of the patriot described in the blank to the right. Choose from the patriots listed at the bottom of the page.

1. A Polish aristocrat who fought on the side of the colonists _____

2. Leader who became second president of the United States _____

3. Famous for the quotation, "Give me liberty or give me death." _____

4. The first man killed in the Boston Massacre _____

5. Her real name was Mary McCauley. She followed her husband to war and reportedly fought when he was wounded. _____

6. A seamstress who made several flags for the revolution _____

7. Wrote the Declaration of Independence _____

8. Naval officer who defeated the British on the sea _____

9. Convinced France to aid the colonists _____

10. Warned the colonists that the British were attacking _____

11. The statesman who was the first to sign the Declaration of Independence

_____

12. She stayed with her husband during the hard winter at Valley Forge. Eventually she became the country's First Lady. _____

13. He led the independence movement in Massachusetts. He organized the Committees of Correspondence. _____

14. General who became the first president of the United States _____

15. He condemned the writs of assistance and said that acts passed by Parliament against the rights of the colonists were invalid. _____

16. Raised money and supervised the finances of the war _____

17. Frenchman who was Washington's aide _____

18. Wrote *Common Sense,* which encouraged independence _____

19. He led a group of men against the British into the west and captured forts at Kaskaskia and Cahokia. _____

20. German officer who helped train American soldiers _____

21. She dressed as a man and enlisted using the name Robert Shurtleff. _____

22. A German-born officer who was killed at the Battle of Camden _____

John Adams, Samuel Adams, Crispus Attucks, George Rogers Clark, Benjamin Franklin, John Hancock, Patrick Henry, Thomas Jefferson, John Paul Jones, Johann de Kalb, Marquis de Lafayette, Molly Pitcher, Casimir Pulaski, Robert Morris, James Otis, Thomas Paine, Paul Revere, Betsy Ross, Deborah Samson, Baron Friedrich von Steuben, George Washington, Martha Washington

Name: _____   Date: _____

Separated by a Common Language

How might life in America be different if the British had won the Revolutionary War? One obvious difference would be the way we speak. While the United States and Britain speak the same language, it is sometimes difficult to understand each other. This is due to the fact that each country uses certain expressions or words that have different meanings in the other country. Listed below are a number of British words or phrases. In the blank to the right, list the word or phrase used in the United States that has the same meaning.

BRITISH EXPRESSION	AMERICAN EXPRESSION	BRITISH EXPRESSION	AMERICAN EXPRESSION
1. Cinema	_____	27. Gaol	_____
2. Yanks	_____	28. Ladybird	_____
3. Flat	_____	29. Barrister	_____
4. School leaver	_____	30. Lead	_____
5. Panda car	_____	31. Number plate	_____
6. Dear	_____	32. Fancy	_____
7. Row	_____	33. Post	_____
8. Ring	_____	34. Diary	_____
9. Water closet	_____	35. Chemist	_____
10. Accumulator	_____	36. Blotto	_____
11. Minder	_____	37. Bobby	_____
12. Tin	_____	38. Ice lolly	_____
13. Cabinet Maker	_____	39. Interval	_____
14. Biscuit	_____	40. Aluminium	_____
15. Anticlockwise	_____	41. Hire	_____
16. Pudding	_____	42. Lad	_____
17. Napkin	_____	43. Pinch	_____
18. Lift	_____	44. Daft	_____
19. Tap	_____	45. Braces	_____
20. Football	_____	46. Boot	_____
21. Sparky	_____	47. Telly	_____
22. Torch	_____	48. Fortnight	_____
23. Chips	_____	49. Holiday	_____
24. Bloke	_____	50. Bloody	_____
25. Bonnet	_____	51. Garden	_____
26. Public school	_____	52. Pavement	_____

Use these words: **Aluminum, Americans, Apartment, Appointment book, Arrest, Babysitter, Bathroom, Battery, Boy, Call, Can, Car hood, Carpenter, Cookie, Counterclockwise, Dessert, Diaper, Dropout, Drunk, Electrician, Elevator, Expensive, Faucet, Flashlight, French fries, Guy, Intermission, Jail, Ladybug, Lawyer, Leash, License plate, Like, Mail, Movie Theatre, Pharmacist, Police car, Policeman, Popsicle, Private school, Quarrel, Rent, Sidewalk, Soccer, Stupid, Suspenders, Trunk, Two weeks, TV, Vacation, Very, Yard**

The War of 1812

The Louisiana Purchase was the most important event in the presidency of Thomas Jefferson. Under Jefferson, the United States more than doubled in size. Perhaps more importantly, the Jefferson presidency was marked by peace and prosperity. Europe, on the other hand, was not so fortunate. France and England were at war, and the United States wanted to remain neutral. But the United States was often caught in the middle. If a U.S. trading ship would sail for Europe, it might be seized and boarded by the British. British sailors would search the ship, and if they found food or supplies being shipped to a French port, they would take the cargo. In some cases, they even took English-born sailors from the American ships and made them serve on British ships. It was not only the British, though, that seized, searched, and took cargo from American ships. The French did it, too.

While the actions of both countries enraged Americans, it was the British that angered them more. The British captured more than twice as many trading ships as the French. Also, Americans were angry because they felt the British were encouraging Indians to attack American settlements on the frontier. In addition, some Americans living in the Northwest Territory wanted to claim more land in Canada that belonged to Britain. For all of these reasons, the United States declared war on Britain in 1812.

Most of the land fighting of the War of 1812 occurred along the Canadian border, in the Chesapeake Bay region, and along the Gulf of Mexico. There was also considerable fighting that took place at sea. In fact, one of the most famous American warships, the *U.S.S. Constitution* fought in this war. The *Constitution* was called, "Old Ironsides." One of the *Constitution's* greatest victories was over the *Guerriere* in the War of 1812.

The British army was successful as they fought in the Northwest Territory. They captured Detroit and were intending to cross into the United States when Captain Oliver Perry intercepted the British on Lake Erie. Although Perry's crews were recently trained and they were sailing homemade ships, they defeated the British fleet, and the United States retained possession of the Northwest Territory.

After the British were defeated in the Northwest, they landed in Chesapeake Bay and marched to Washington, D.C. They set fire to the U.S. Capitol, the president's home, and other government buildings. After the war, the president's home was repaired and painted white. That is why it is called the White House today.

The British army left Washington and went to Baltimore. As the British ships were firing on Fort McHenry in Baltimore Harbor, Francis Scott Key was on board one of the British ships. He was trying to get the British to release an American prisoner. As Key watched the fort being attacked, he wrote a poem that was later set to music. Today that poem is the national anthem of the United States. It is called the *Star-Spangled Banner*.

The last major battle of the war was fought after the peace treaty was signed. It was called the Battle of New Orleans. The treaty was signed in Ghent, in what is now Belgium, and word of it did not reach the United States before the British attacked New Orleans. Andrew Jackson commanded the American troops in this battle and was successful over the British.

Name: _____ Date: _____

War of 1812 Quiz

Shown below are a number of sentences. Some are true and some are false. If the sentence is true, write the word "true" in front of the sentence. If the sentence is false, write a term that could replace the term written in bold type to make the sentence true.

_____ 1. Under President **Jackson**, the United States more than doubled in size.

_____ 2. The War of 1812 was fought between the United States and **France**.

_____ 3. The battleship *Constitution* was called "**Old Ironsides**."

_____ 4. The last major battle of the War of 1812 was the Battle of **Bunker Hill**.

_____ 5. The U.S. leader at the Battle of New Orleans was Andrew **Jefferson**.

_____ 6. The treaty ending the War of 1812 is called the Treaty of **Ghent**.

_____ 7. During the assault on Ft. McHenry, Francis Scott **Key** wrote a poem that became our national anthem.

_____ 8. Today, Key's poem is called the **"Battle Hymn of the Republic."**

_____ 9. The British set fire to the U.S. **Capitol**.

_____ 10. When the president's home was repaired it was painted **beige**.

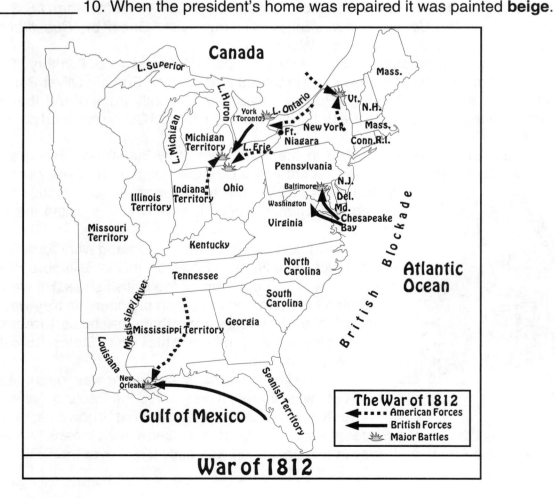

Name: _____ Date: _____

The Star-Spangled Banner

During the War of 1812, Francis Scott Key, a young American lawyer and poet, boarded a British frigate as the British bombarded Fort McHenry in Baltimore, Maryland. Key went aboard the ship under a flag of truce. He was trying to arrange for the release of a prisoner held by the British. The British kept Key on board during the attack. As Key watched the attack, he was so moved with emotion that he wrote a poem about the experience. He called the poem "Defense of Fort McHenry." The poem was printed in a handbill, and then it was printed in a Baltimore newspaper. People began singing the poem to the tune of a well-known drinking song by Englishman, John Stafford Smith. Eventually the poem with the music was published under the title, *The Star-Spangled Banner,* and it became very popular. On March 3, 1931, Congress made the song our official national anthem.

While most Americans love the song and sing it frequently at sporting events and other occasions, some people have criticized it. They say the song is too difficult for most people to sing. The song begins in a relatively easy range but then later moves to higher notes, which many people are unable to sing. Many of these critics feel that the national anthem of the United States should be *America the Beautiful.*

The Star-Spangled Banner has several verses, but the first verse is the best known:

> Oh, say, can you see, by the dawn's early light,
> What so proudly we hail'd at the twilight's last gleaming?
> Whose broad stripes and bright stars, thro' the perilous fight,
> O'er the ramparts we watch'd, were so gallantly streaming?
> And the rockets' red glare, the bombs bursting in air,
> Gave proof thro' the night that our flag was still there.
> Oh, say, does that star-spangled banner yet wave
> O'er the land of the free and the home of the brave?

Shown below are several pictures. Underneath each picture write the *phrase* from the *Star-Spangled Banner* that the picture illustrates.

1._____ 2._____ 3._____

47

Name: _____ Date: _____

4._____

5._____

6._____

7._____

8._____

9._____

_____

10._____

11._____

Florida Purchase From Spain in 1819

When the United States purchased Louisiana from France, the boundaries between Louisiana and Florida, which was owned by Spain, were not clearly defined in the treaty. The United States thought that part of the purchase of Louisiana included a strip of land along the Gulf of Mexico called West Florida. On the surface, the land did not seem important. It was mostly swamp and forest. The United States, however, felt ownership of this land was important for several reasons:

1. The United States purchased Louisiana from France to control the Mississippi in order to ship goods and products to Europe without interference. West Florida, the contested strip of land, bordered the Mississippi close to its mouth.
2. The land contained good harbors.
3. Spain was openly hostile to the U.S. government and to the U.S. settlers close to Florida. They armed the Seminole Indians so they could attack Americans. They also permitted Britain to station troops in Florida during the War of 1812.
4. The forest and swamp, coupled with the hostile attitude of the Spaniards for the United States, made the area a haven for runaway slaves and criminals.

The ownership of this area was disputed for many years. Gradually, the United States occupied it, and when Louisiana was admitted as a state in 1812, the U.S. government claimed West Florida as part of the United States.

That, of course, did not solve all the problems between the United States and Florida. Slaves and criminals were still escaping and hiding in Florida. Seminole Indians from Florida were still raiding settlements in the United States. So, President Monroe sent General Andrew Jackson to put an end to the Indian raids. Jackson went beyond his instructions. He pursued the Indians into Florida and captured two Spanish forts. President Monroe returned the forts to the Spanish and ordered Jackson to withdraw his troops.

Jackson's invasion into Florida, however, made it clear that Spain could not defend the colony. So in 1819, Spain sold Florida to the United States for $5,000,000. The treaty that transferred ownership of Florida from Spain to the United States also required that the United States give up claims to Texas, which some argued was a part of the Louisiana Purchase. Spain was required to give up claims to the Oregon Country. Florida became a state in 1845.

The strip of land below Mississippi and Alabama and above West Florida had been disputed after the Treaty of 1783. The treaty set the northern boundary of Florida much lower than Spain felt it should be, and since Spain was not involved in the negotiations, she did not feel she had to comply. In 1795, the area was ceded to the United States.

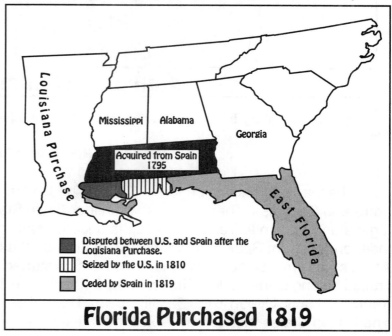

Florida Purchased 1819

War With Mexico

Early Spanish explorations of the Americas enabled Spain to claim a great deal of the newly-discovered continents, although most of Spain's interest was in Central and South America. With the exception of Florida, Spain had little interest in settling in North America until the eighteenth century. Spain decided settlements in the Southwest would secure the area. Spain was concerned that the French, who owned the Louisiana Territory in the early part of the eighteenth century, would expand westward, annexing land that belonged to Spain. So Spanish settlements began to appear in what is now the state of Texas. Spain was also concerned that Russia and England, who at this time claimed land north of Spanish Territory, might expand south to what is now California and claim this area for their countries. So Spanish settlements were started in what is now California to strengthen Spain's claim to the territory.

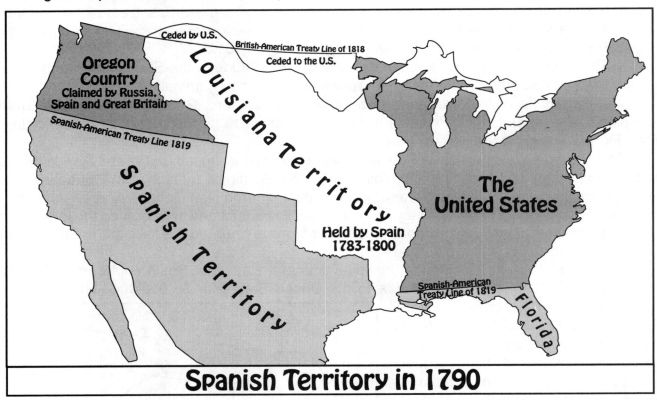

Spanish Territory in North America in 1790. Spain claimed land far south into Central and South America.

TEXAS WAR FOR INDEPENDENCE

The war with Mexico began in Texas. The United States had claimed Texas as part of the Louisiana Purchase. Then, in 1819, when the United States signed the Florida Treaty with Spain, it gave up its claim to Texas, and Texas became part of Mexico. In 1821, Mexico declared itself independent from Spain and claimed all of the land the Spanish had colonized, including Texas. At the same time, settlers from the United States started moving into this area and felt that it really should belong to the United States. Many felt that it was the destiny of the United States to extend from the Atlantic Ocean to the Pacific Ocean. This philosophy was referred to as **Manifest Destiny**. The United States tried to buy Texas, but Mexico refused.

By 1830, there were more American settlers in Texas than Mexicans. So Mexico passed a law forbidding any more Americans from settling in Texas. They also passed laws that affected the rights of the settlers and their ability to govern themselves. As a result, in 1835, Texas declared its independence from Mexico. Mexico moved to stop Texas from seceding from Mexico with armed soldiers. The Mexican army was successful in two battles, but lost the final battle.

The first and most famous defeat of the Texans occurred at the Alamo, a Spanish Mission. One hundred eighty-seven Texans, including Jim Bowie and Davy Crockett, locked themselves in the Alamo, and for 11 days held off a siege by 3,000 Mexicans. The Mexicans, led by General Santa Anna, won, and all of the Texans were killed. Shortly after the Alamo, Mexican forces overpowered and executed the Texan defenders of Goliad. However, a few weeks later, the Texans, led by Sam Houston, defeated the Mexicans in the battle of San Jacinto. As a result of this battle, Texas became the Lone Star Republic of Texas.

Texas remained an independent republic for 10 years. Many wanted Texas to be annexed to the United States. Southerners felt that since Texas had so many cotton farmers who used slaves, slavery could be extended. In fact, Texas was large enough to make several slave states. These very reasons caused Northerners to oppose the annexation of Texas. Northerners also argued that since Mexico never acknowledged Texas's independence, annexation would cause a war between the two countries.

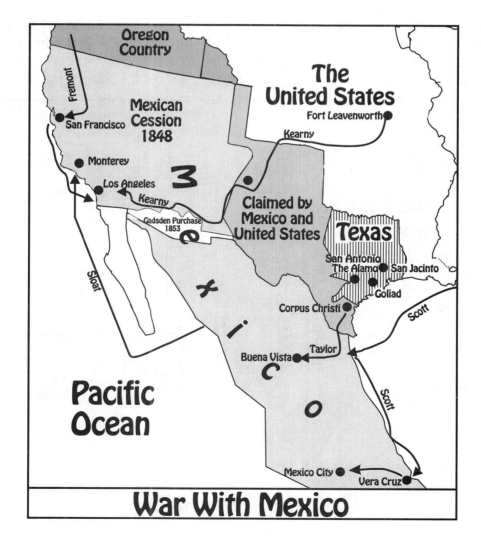

War With Mexico

MEXICAN-AMERICAN WAR

In 1845, Texas was admitted to the Union, and as many had predicted, this led to war with Mexico. Not only had the United States angered Mexico by annexing Texas, but there was a dispute over the southern boundary line of Texas. Texas claimed that the Rio Grande River marked the southern boundary of Texas. Mexico said the land between the Nueces River and the Rio Grande, an area of about 100 miles in width, was not part of Texas. In 1846, President Polk sent Zachary Taylor to Texas to defend the disputed border. Mexican forces attacked the troops, and Congress declared war on Mexico.

The war lasted two years. General Scott captured Vera Cruz and then captured Mexico City. While the war was waging in the South, American soldiers occupied California. A peace treaty was signed between the two countries in 1848. As a result of the treaty:

- Mexico recognized Texas as part of the United States.
- The border between Mexico and the United States was established at the Rio Grande River.
- Mexico gave up her claim to all of the Southwest Territory to the Pacific Ocean. This is the area that now makes up the states of California, Utah, New Mexico, Arizona, Nevada, and parts of Colorado and Wyoming.
- The United States agreed to pay $15,000,000 for the land and $3,500,000 to American citizens for debts that were owed to them by Mexico.

In 1853, the United States bought a small parcel of land from Mexico that extended the southern boundaries of New Mexico and Arizona. This was called the Gadsden Purchase after James Gadsden, the U.S. ambassador to Mexico. The land was purchased to build a southern transcontinental railroad. The United States paid Mexico $10,000,000 for the land.

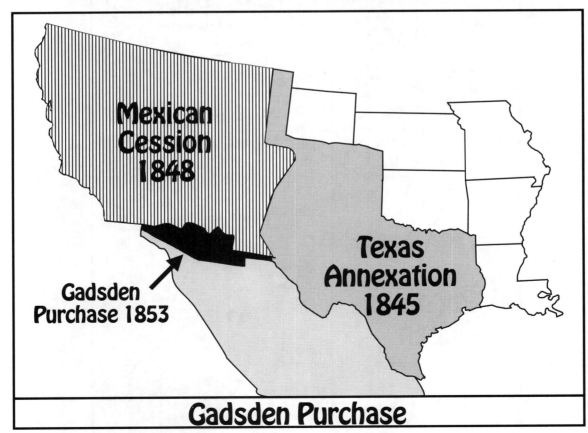

Gadsden Purchase

Name: _____ Date: _____

War With Mexico Puzzle

During the eighteenth century, Americans came to believe the whole continent should belong to the United States. This philosophy was the cause of wars with Mexico as well as clashes and treaties with other countries. This philosophy had a name. If you fill in the puzzle below, the philosophy will be spelled out in the circles as you read down the page.

1.
2.
3.
4.
5.
6.
7.
8.
9.
10.
11.
12.
13.
14.
15.

Answer the following questions and fill in the answers in the grid above.

1. In 1835, Texas declared its independence from _____.
2. The first and most famous defeat of the Texans occurred at a Spanish mission called the _____ .
3. The United States claimed Texas as part of the _____.
4. The_____ River forms the border between Texas and Mexico.
5. The United States purchased the Louisiana Territory from the _____.
6. _____ City is the capital of Mexico.
7. In 1819, the United States purchased Florida from_____.
8. After the Texas war for independence, _____ remained a republic for 10 years before it became a state.
9. In 1853, the United States bought a small parcel of land that extended the southern boundaries of New Mexico and Arizona. This was called the_____ Purchase.
10. _____ was president when the United States bought Florida from Spain.
11. General Andrew _____ led troops into Florida to stop Indian raids.
12. After the war with Mexico, Texas became the Lone _____ Republic of Texas.
13. The United States thought that part of the purchase of Louisiana included a strip of land along the Gulf of Mexico called West _____.
14. The name of the Mexican General who defeated the Texans at the Alamo was _____ _____ .
15. A Tennessee frontiersman who died at the Alamo was _____.
16. The philosophy spelled out in the puzzle is: _____

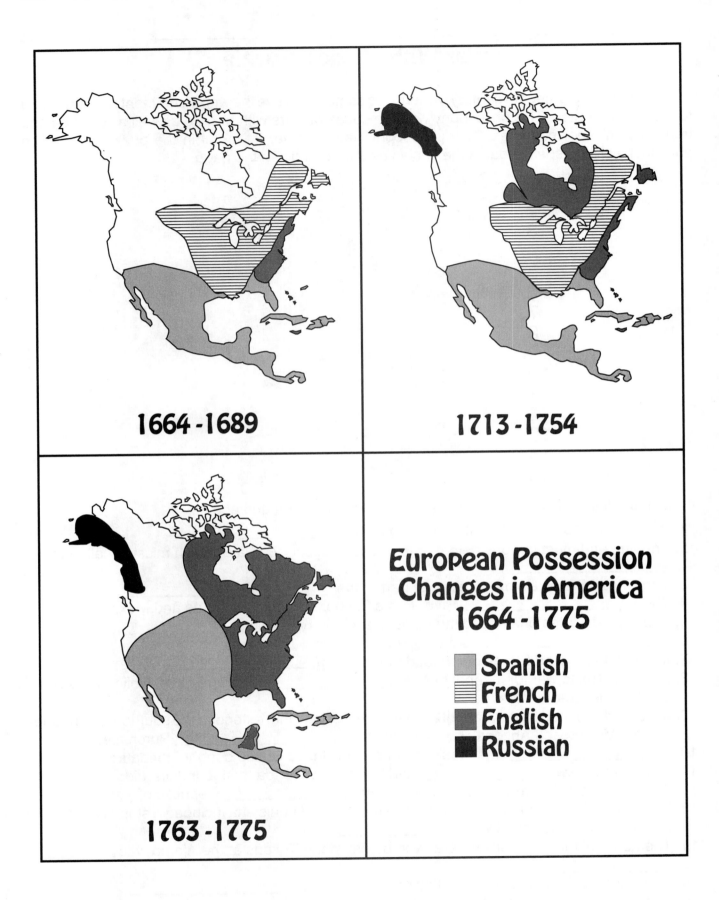

1664 - 1689

1713 - 1754

1763 - 1775

European Possession Changes in America 1664 - 1775

Spanish
French
English
Russian

The United States in 1783

When the Revolutionary War ended, one of the things the new government had to deal with was the organization of the western territories. Boundaries of the states had not been accurately surveyed. Several states had argued for years that the boundaries of their states extended from the coast all the way to the Mississippi River. Other states claimed other territories as part of their own states. These claims were based on their original "sea to sea" colonial charters and also from grants from Indians. What made the situation even more confusing was the fact that many of the claims overlapped. On the other hand, some states made no claims on the western lands, but felt they should have access to the West.

This was a serious problem for the Continental Congress as the representatives drew up the Articles of Confederation for their new nation. The states without western claims argued that possession of the West came as a result of a cooperative effort by all of the colonies, and when Great Britain gave up this territory by the Treaty of 1783, the land belonged to all states, not just some of them. The two sides argued.

The problem was eventually solved by Maryland, who refused to ratify the Articles of Confederation unless the disputed western territories were ceded back to the federal government. Maryland felt the western lands should form a public domain, controlled by the government. Maryland further suggested that the land be sold to settlers. Selling land to the settlers would benefit the Union in two ways. It would not only increase the Federal Treasury, it would encourage people to move and settle in these western territories. With an increasing population, new states would be formed, strengthening the country. Maryland's suggestion was adopted, and within a few years after the Articles of Confederation were adopted, most of the disputed lands were turned over to the United States, reducing the eastern states to their present boundaries.

Name: _____ Date: _____

Are You From Virginia?

Are you from Virginia? Before you answer that question, remember that after the Revolutionary War, several states laid claim to western territories based on their original colonial charters and on Indian grants. This is one of the difficult issues the Continental Congress needed to resolve. Eventually, most of the disputed lands were turned over to the federal government, setting the present boundaries of the states. But what would have happened if the territories had not been ceded back? What if the territory actually became part of the state that claimed it?

Compare a map showing the claims to western territories made by the states in 1783 (page 55) with a current U.S. map. On the current map, locate the cities listed below and determine which state they would be in today if the territories had not been ceded to the federal government. Before each city are the letters "C," which represents Connecticut, "G," which represents Georgia, "M," which represents Massachusetts, "N," which represents North Carolina, and "V," which represents Virginia. Circle the letter of the state where the city would be if the western claims had remained as they were in 1783.

C G M V N   1. Montgomery, Alabama
C G M V N   2. Chicago, Illinois
C G M V N   3. Madison, Wisconsin
C G M V N   4. Indianapolis, Indiana
C G M V N   5. Toledo, Ohio
C G M V N   6. Portland, Maine
C G M V N   7. Springfield, Illinois
C G M V N   8. Jackson, Mississippi
C G M V N   9. Lexington, Kentucky
C G M V N   10. Cleveland, Ohio
C G M V N   11. Nashville, Tennessee
C G M V N   12. Gary, Indiana
C G M V N   13. Cincinnati, Ohio
C G M V N   14. Akron, Ohio
C G M V N   15. Knoxville, Tennessee
C G M V N   16. South Bend, Indiana
C G M V N   17. Memphis, Tennessee
C G M V N   18. Birmingham, Alabama
C G M V N   19. Hartford, Connecticut
C G M V N   20. Buffalo, New York
C G M V N   21. Rochester, New York
C G M V N   22. Rock Island, Illinois
C G M V N   23. St. Paul, Minnesota
C G M V N   24. Charleston, West Virginia
C G M V N   25. Paducah, Kentucky

Indian Relocation: Trail of Tears

After the Revolutionary War, the population of the United States steadily increased and expanded westward. Many settled in Georgia, the land of the Native Cherokee. The Cherokee learned a great deal from the newcomers. The Cherokee were farmers and ranchers who built roads, schools, and churches. They developed a representational government patterned after the United States and had an alphabet. But while the Cherokee had learned from the Europeans who had come to their land, they suffered as well. More than half of the Cherokee people died as a result of smallpox epidemics brought by the Europeans. The Revolutionary War caused the Cherokee to lose another quarter of their population. Now these settlers wanted their land.

Between 1733 and 1830, both the Cherokee and the Creek Indians had ceded several parcels of land to the government. This land was made available to white settlers who began moving into the region. In 1830 the last bit of land controlled by the Cherokee was in northern Georgia. In that year, the Congress of the United States passed the "Indian Removal Act," which President Jackson signed into law. The Cherokees challenged the removal law in the Supreme Court and won. The Supreme Court said the Cherokee nation had to sign a treaty agreeing to the removal before it became legal. However, Georgia did not obey the Supreme Court ruling and continued with a lottery to give the Indian land to the white settlers. While most Cherokees still did not want to sign a treaty and be removed from their land, a small minority of Cherokees agreed and signed a treaty for removal from their land in exchange for five million dollars. The treaty was ratified by the Congress of the United States.

On May 17, 1838, General Winfield Scott arrived in Georgia with 7,000 men and began the process of rounding up the Cherokees and taking them to Oklahoma. Since the treaty was not signed by the elected representatives of the Cherokee, most refused to leave. They were arrested and placed in forts with little food. The Cherokee people were then forced to march 1,000 miles to their new home. The conditions were terrible and about 4,000 died as a result of the march.

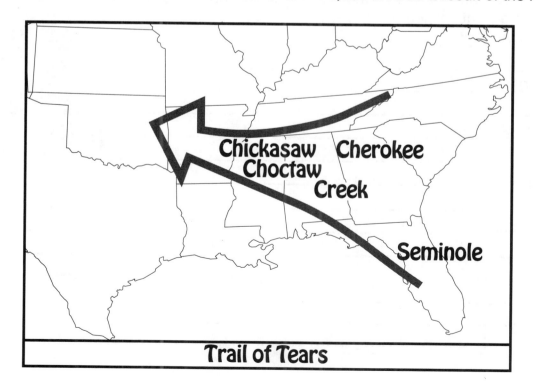

Trail of Tears

Name: _____   Date: _____

Indian Relocation: Points of View

Since U.S. history has been written, for the most part, by descendants of European settlers, little attention has been given to the culture of the Native Americans who were living in America for thousands of years before the Europeans arrived. Give your reactions to the relocation of the Cherokee Indians from their land in Georgia to Oklahoma from different points of view. First explain the event as if you were a white settler moving into the area. Then describe the same event as if you were a Cherokee being moved.

1. Views of the White Settler: _____

_____

_____

_____

2. Views of the Cherokee: _____

_____

_____

_____

Famous Native Americans

Listed below are just a few famous Native Americans. Find out about them and write what you learn in the space below.

1. Red Cloud _____

_____

2. Sitting Bull _____

_____

3. Crazy Horse _____

_____

4. Sacajewea _____

_____

5. Will Rogers _____

_____

6. Jim Thorpe _____

_____

7. Pocahontas _____

_____

Name: _____ Date: _____

The Northwest Ordinance of 1787

Not long after the Revolutionary War, many settlers moved west to live on the frontier. Many settled in an area called the Northwest Territory. The Northwest Territory was the area east of the Mississippi and north of the Ohio River. This land belonged to the federal government, and the government passed a law called the Northwest Ordinance of 1787. This law is one of the most important in the history of United States. It developed a pattern of government for U.S. territories. When the territory was small, the territory would be governed by a governor and three judges appointed by Congress. When there were 5,000 free, adult men living in the territory, they could elect an assembly to govern them. Whenever the population reached 600,000, the area could become a state. The ordinance also provided that:

1. The Northwest Territory would eventually be organized into not more than five, nor less than three, states.
2. Once the states were formed, they were to be admitted to the Union and its citizens were to have rights equal to those residing in the original states.
3. Slavery would be excluded from the territory.
4. Schools and education would be encouraged.
5. There would be freedom of religion.

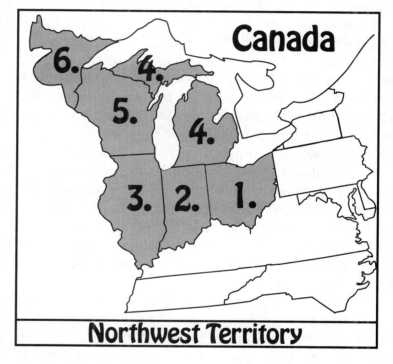

The most important aspect of the Northwest Ordinance was that it developed a pattern for other land and territories acquired by the United States either by war or by treaty. As settlers moved into these newly-acquired lands, the Northwest Ordinance was a guide for development and for government.

Identify States Developed from the Northwest Territory

On the lines below, identify the five complete states and the one partial state developed from the Northwest Territory. Also, write the name of each state's capital. Label each of the Great Lakes on the map.

1._____   4._____

2._____   5._____

3._____   6._____

Louisiana Purchase

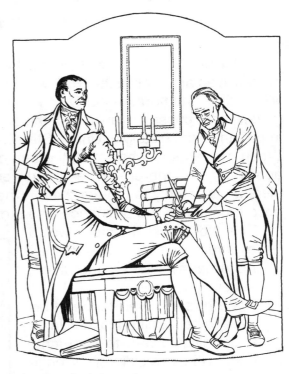

The area known as Louisiana extended from Canada on the north to the Gulf of Mexico on the south, and from the Mississippi River on the east to the Rocky Mountains on the west. It was originally claimed for France by the French explorer La Salle and other early explorers. As a result of the French and Indian War, which ended with the Treaty of Paris in 1763, Louisiana was given to Spain. However, France got Louisiana back by a secret treaty in 1800. When the United States found out the French had regained control of the area, Americans were upset. They felt they had nothing to fear when Spain owned Louisiana since Spain was not a very strong country. But France was another matter. France already owned New Orleans, which was on the east side of the Mississippi River, and if it owned Louisiana, it could control the Mississippi, which America used to send goods to Europe. Many Americans were so concerned that they were ready to go to war to protect the outlet for their goods.

President Jefferson pursued a more peaceful solution. He sent representatives to France to buy New Orleans and an area to the east between the Gulf of Mexico and the United States. The representatives met with Napoleon to make the purchase. At first, Napoleon refused. He wanted to colonize the area and build a French empire in North America. Abruptly, Napoleon changed his mind. He decided not to sell just New Orleans, but to sell all of Louisiana. Napoleon did not have troops to defend the territory, and he was close to a renewed war with Great Britain. He also needed money for his military operations.

So, by a treaty signed in 1803, the United States purchased Louisiana from France for 60 million francs, or about $15 million. The area included the western half of the Mississippi valley and the Island of Orleans. The purchase added over 800,000 square miles of area to the United States. At the time of the purchase, Jefferson said, that with the stroke of the pen by signing the treaty, we "more than doubled the area of the United States."

The boundaries for Louisiana were not as clearly defined as shown in the map on page 61. Spain claimed that its territory included part of what is now Texas. And although not a part of the Louisiana Purchase, Spain also felt that its possessions reached well northward into Oregon Country. The United States felt Texas and West Florida east to the Perdido River were part of the Louisiana Purchase. The dispute lasted for several years after the Louisiana Purchase. Between 1810 and 1814, the United States seized the disputed area known as West Florida. In 1819, the United States signed a treaty with Spain. Under this treaty, Spain was paid $5,000,000. In return, Spain gave up its claim to East and West Florida. Spain also gave up any claims to the territory on the Pacific coast north of the forty-second parallel. A boundary of Spain's territory was also established on the south and east, which included what is now the state of Texas. In other words, the treaty gave Florida to the United States, and Spain got Texas. In addition, the boundaries for the United States and Spain were clearly defined.

Name: _____ Date: _____

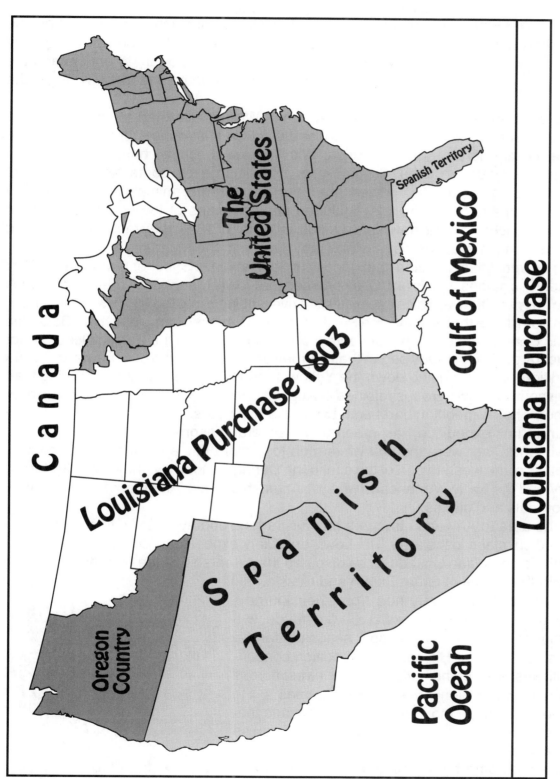

Identify States Developed From the Louisiana Purchase

On the map shown:
1. Identify and label the thirteen states either wholly are partially developed from the Louisiana Purchase.
2. Write the date each state was admitted to the Union.
3. Locate the capital of each state, write its name, and mark it with a star.

The Lewis and Clark Expedition

Although the United States was eager to purchase Louisiana, not much was known about the area. Once the territory belonged to the United States, President Thomas Jefferson moved quickly to send exploring parties to the West to learn more about it. It was important to understand the geography of the area as well as develop friendly relations with the Native Americans living in the region.

In 1804, two explorers named Meriwether Lewis and William Clark led an expedition into Louisiana. Lewis was Jefferson's private secretary and Clark was a younger brother of George Rogers Clark, the military hero of the Revolution. With a crew of scouts, hunters, cooks, and workers, they began their journey up the Missouri River in three large row boats. As they traveled, they wrote about their journey in diaries and described all of the plant life, animals, and natives they encountered. Their journals, or diaries, also included detailed maps of the country they were exploring. When they reached what is now North Dakota in the fall of 1804, they met and befriended the Mandan Indians living in the area. That winter they lived with the Mandans.

When spring arrived, the expedition continued with Sacajawea, a Shoshone woman, and her husband, a fur trader, as guides. Lewis and Clark crossed the Rocky Mountains. Their journey took them past the **Continental Divide,** which separates the rivers flowing into the Mississippi River and the Gulf of Mexico from those that flow into the Pacific Ocean. They then came down the Columbia River to the Pacific Ocean. It had taken them a year and a half to reach the Pacific Ocean. After spending the winter by the Pacific, they began their journey back in March of 1806. Lewis and Clark split up the expedition, with one going down the Yellowstone River and the other retracing their route down the Missouri. The two groups rejoined in August, and the expedition arrived back in St. Louis in September. Their expedition had taken two and a half years.

The Lewis and Clark expedition was important for several reasons:

- Since Lewis and Clark were the first white men to explore this area, it gave the country specific details of the western part of the continent. During the journey, they not only studied the country and the Native Americans who inhabited this region, they recorded what they found in journals and diaries.
- It opened the area to American trappers and fur-traders, and eventually, to settlers.
- It established our claim to the area. The Lewis and Clark expedition would become an important factor as the United States disputed the ownership of the Oregon Country with the claims of Great Britain and Russia.

The year Lewis and Clark returned from their journey, Zebulon N. Pike was sent west to explore. Pike made two important expeditions. On his first expedition, he looked for the source of the Mississippi River. His second expedition concentrated on the Southwest area of the nation. He went west across Kansas, and then traveled along the Rocky Mountains. He discovered, but did not climb, a mountain peak in Colorado that was named in his honor. He then turned south into Spanish territory, where he was arrested. After a short while, he was released, and he went home by traveling through Texas and Louisiana. Pike's expeditions were valuable in understanding the resources of the southwestern part of the Louisiana Purchase.

Name: _____ Date: _____

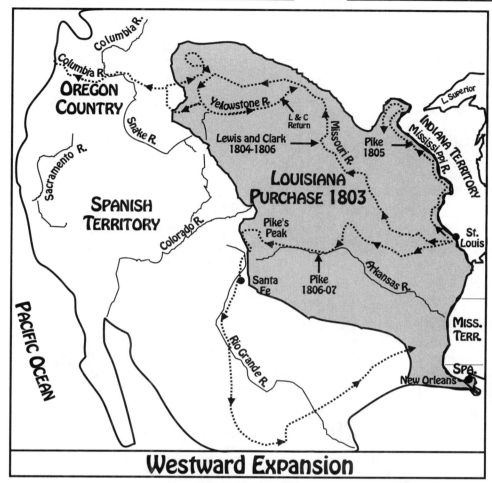

Westward Expansion

Lewis and Clark Quiz

Shown below are a number of sentences. Some are true and some are false. If the sentence is true, write the word "true" in front of the sentence. If the sentence is false, write a term that could replace the term written in bold type to make the sentence true.

_____ 1. President Jefferson sent explorers to learn more about the land the United States acquired through the **Civil War**.

_____ 2. **Lewis and Clark** led an expedition into the Louisiana Territory.

_____ 3. Lewis and Clark began their journey on the **Mississippi** River.

_____ 4. Lewis and Clark's journey took them past the **Continental Divide**.

_____ 5. Pike's Peak was named after **Zebulon N. Peak.**

_____ 6. On Pike's first expedition, he looked for the source of the **Missouri**.

_____ 7. In the winter, Lewis and Clark lived with the **Sioux** Indians.

_____ 8. Lewis and Clark's expedition began in **1800.**

_____ 9. Lewis and Clark's expedition lasted **4½** years.

_____ 10. Pike's exploration was important to understand the resources of the **northwestern** part of the Louisiana Purchase.

         63

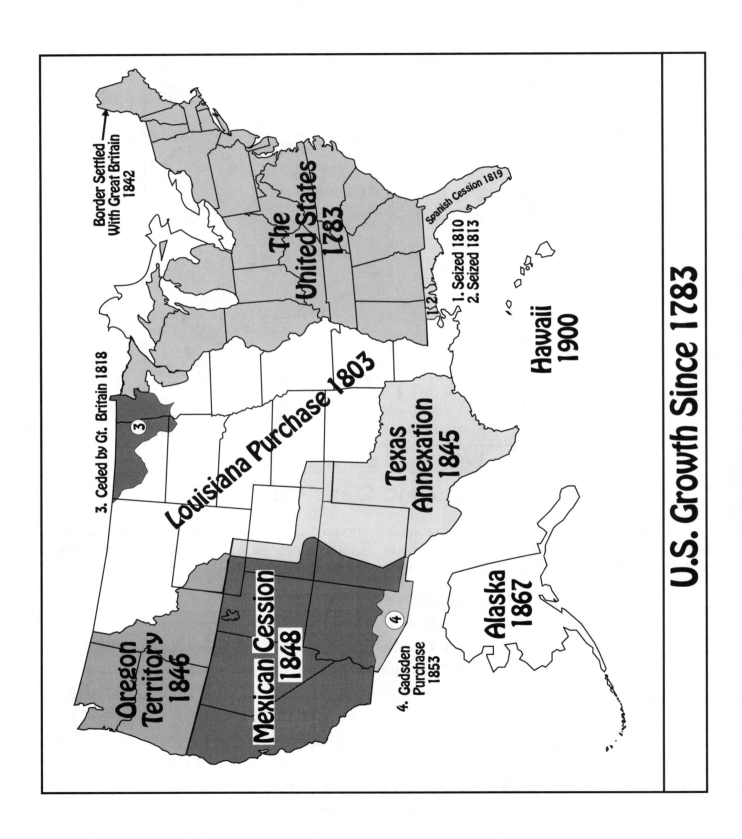

U.S. Growth Since 1783

Border Settled With Great Britain 1842

The United States 1783

Spanish Cession 1819

1. Seized 1810
2. Seized 1813

Hawaii 1900

3. Ceded by Gt. Britain 1818

Louisiana Purchase 1803

Texas Annexation 1845

Oregon Territory 1846

Mexican Cession 1848

Alaska 1867

4. Gadsden Purchase 1853

Name: _____ Date: _____

Growth of the United States Quiz

Refer to the map on page 64. How and when were the following areas, which later became the following states, acquired by the United States?

1. California _____

2. Florida _____

3. Washington _____

4. Arkansas _____

5. Texas _____

6. Louisiana _____

7. Nebraska _____

8. Idaho _____

9. Utah _____

10. South Dakota _____

Shown below are a number of sentences. Some are true and some are false. If the sentence is true, write the word "true" in front of the sentence. If the sentence is false, write a term that could replace the term written in bold type to make the sentence true.

_____ 11. The United States grew from **west** to **east**.

_____ 12. The **Gadsden** Purchase was the largest addition of territory to the United States.

_____ 13. The land east of the Appalachian Mountains was acquired as a result of the **Civil** War.

_____ 14. The Louisiana Territory was purchased from **Spain**.

_____ 15. California was added to the Union as a result of the **Revolutionary** War.

_____ 16. The Gadsden Purchase was land that was owned by **Mexico**.

_____ 17. Part of North Dakota once belonged to **Great Britain**.

_____ 18. The Oregon Country was eventually made into three whole states. They were Washington, Oregon, and **California**.

_____ 19. Florida was purchased from the **Seminoles**.

_____ 20. Oregon and **Florida** were acquired about the same time.

_____ 21. Part of two states resulted from a treaty in 1818 between the United States and Great Britain. They were North Dakota and **Michigan**.

_____ 22. **Hawaii** was purchased from Russia.

_____ 23. The last territory acquired by the United States was the **Oregon** Territory.

_____ 24. The **Oregon Country** was added to the United States in 1803.

_____ 25. Most of the land in the United States was acquired **before** 1800.

Trails Leading Westward

Trappers and traders began traveling west to the Pacific Ocean. Over the years, the routes they traveled became recognized trails that settlers and others would eventually use as they made their journeys across the continent. These trails became so well-known, that forts were built along them. Settlers using these trails could stop at these forts for supplies. In 1848, these trails became very important. It was in this year that gold was discovered in California and the Gold Rush began. Since most people did not leave for California immediately, but waited until the spring of 1849, they were called the "Forty-Niners."

For those who wanted to get to California in a hurry and were not bothered by the danger, they could sail to the Isthumus of Panama, travel across land to the Pacific Ocean, and catch a boat for San Francisco. This was a very dangerous route because of the swamps and Yellow Fever. So most settlers and Forty-Niners went west over one of the trails that crossed the continent. There were four trails that were more popular than the rest.

OREGON TRAIL

The Oregon Trail was 2,000 miles long and stretched from Independence, Missouri, to the Columbia River in Oregon. The first part of the route followed the Platte River for approximately 540 miles through what is now Nebraska to Fort Laramie in present-day Wyoming. The trail then followed along the North Platte and Sweetwater Rivers to the South Pass in the Wind River Range of the Rocky mountains. The trail then went south to Fort Bridger, Wyoming, and then turned into the Bear River valley and went north to Fort Hall in present-day Idaho. In Idaho, the trail followed the Snake River to the Salmon Falls and then went north past Fort Boise, which is now Boise, Idaho. The trail then entered what is now Oregon, passed through the Grande Ronde River valley, crossed the Blue Mountains, and followed the Umatilla River to the Columbia River.

CALIFORNIA TRAIL

The California Trail followed the Oregon Trail to the Great Salt Lake in Utah and then turned southward through what is now Nevada to California. This was the most direct route to California, but it was very dangerous. Travelers had to cross mountains and deserts. The big risk was being stranded in the mountains during the winter snows.

SANTA FE TRAIL

Santa Fe was an important city in the Spanish Territory and relied on trade to supply its needs. Since Santa Fe was closer to the American frontier than to Mexico City, New Spain's capital, it was only natural that a route between Missouri and Santa Fe would be developed. The Santa Fe Trail began in Independence, Missouri, and led to Santa Fe. It was about 800 miles long. From Santa Fe, travelers going to Los Angeles had two choices. The Desert Trail went south from Santa Fe. It led down to the Mexican border, across southern California, and then north to Los Angeles.

OLD SPANISH TRAIL

Travelers could also choose the Old Spanish Trail. The Old Spanish Trail began in Santa Fe and arched northward through the mountains and over the Colorado River and then went down to Los Angeles.

Name:_____ Date: _____

Which Trail Would You Take?

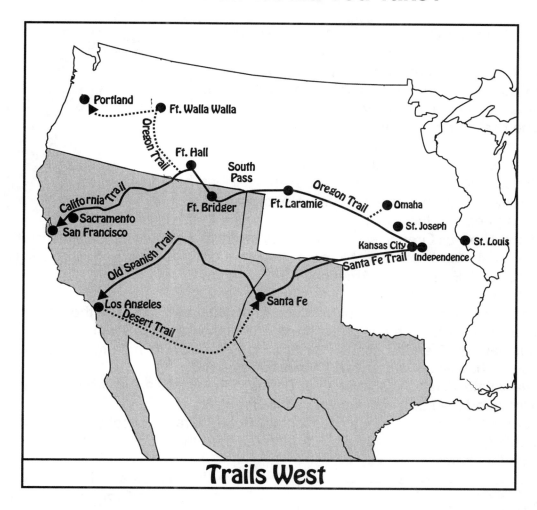

Trails West

List the trails you would take if you were traveling to the following destinations. Some of the cities, of course, did not exist when the trails were being used.

Which trail would you take if ...?

1. You were traveling to Seattle, Washington?_____

2. You were traveling to Sacramento, California?_____

3. You were traveling to Santa Fe, New Mexico?_____

4. You were traveling to Phoenix, Arizona? _____

5. You were traveling to Reno, Nevada? _____

6. You were traveling to Salt Lake City, Utah?_____

7. You were traveling to Albuquerque, New Mexico? _____

8. You were traveling to San Francisco, California? _____

9. You were traveling to San Diego, California?_____

10. You were traveling to Tucson, Arizona? _____

Oregon Country

The area between California and Alaska was called Oregon Country. It was the land north of 42° north latitude and west of the Rocky Mountains. This area included what are now the states of Oregon, Washington, and Idaho. Oregon was discovered in 1792 by Captain Robert Gray. President Thomas Jefferson sent Meriwether Lewis and William Clark to explore Oregon in 1803. By 1818, many Americans were settling in the region, but it was not part of the United States. The Americans settling in the area felt that it should become part of the United States. Congressmen from the west agreed, but the congressmen from the south and east did not. They felt Oregon was too far away from the rest of the United States. Another problem was that Oregon was occupied by both England and America. In fact, Oregon was claimed by four countries.

Four Nations Claimed Oregon Before 1818

- **Spain** felt that it belonged to her because when Balboa discovered the Pacific Ocean, he claimed all of the land that touched the ocean in the name of Spain.
- **Britain** claimed Oregon because Sir Francis Drake, Captain James Cook, and Captain Vancouver had sailed around and explored its coast.
- **Russia** claimed Oregon because Vitus Bering, a Russian, claimed what is now Alaska after he discovered the strait now known as the Bering Strait.
- The **United States** said that since Captain Robert Gray had sailed up the mouth of the Columbia River and Lewis and Clark also reached the mouth of the Columbia, Oregon belonged to them.

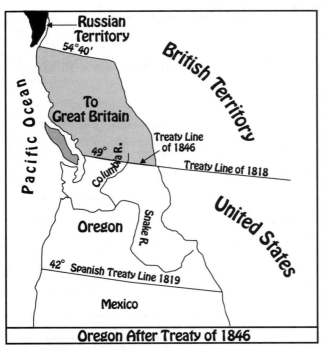

Oregon After Treaty of 1846

The United States had already suggested to Great Britain that the Oregon Territory be divided along the line of 49° north latitude, but Britain refused. The claim by the United States became part of the presidential campaign of 1844. James Polk was elected president by running on a platform that Oregon clearly belonged to the United States and said that he felt the United States should occupy Oregon and annex Texas. Polk also felt that all of Oregon up to Alaska should belong to the United States. Those who supported this idea had a rallying cry, "Fifty-four forty or fight!" This meant that the United States should claim the land up to the Alaskan boundary, which was 54° 40′. In 1846, just before war was to begin between the United States and Mexico, Britain drafted a treaty that divided Oregon on the 49° parallel from the Pacific to the Rockies. It was signed by Britain and the United States. The treaty gave the British Vancouver Island, as well as the right to navigate the Columbia River.

Name:_____ Date: _____

Oregon Country Puzzle

Complete the puzzle below by answering the following questions about Oregon Country. After you have finished the puzzle, read down the circled letters and it will reveal the name of a feature of this territory that played an important role in its discovery and exploration.

1. One of two Americans who explored the area. His first name was William.
2. This president of the United States, elected in 1844, felt that Oregon belonged to the United States.
3. A large state on the Pacific coast, just south of the Oregon Country.
4. Another state south of the Oregon Country. It has a large, salt lake.
5. The Oregon Country is west of the Rocky_____.
6. This country claimed Oregon because Sir Francis Drake and others explored its coast.
7. This country claimed Oregon because Balboa discovered the Pacific Ocean.
8. One of the states made from the Oregon Country.
9. This country claimed Oregon because Vitus Bering claimed Alaska.
10. One of two Americans who explored the area. His first name was Meriwether.
11. The treaty gave this island to Britain.
12. The _____ States also claimed to own the Oregon Country.
13. This captain explored the mouth of the Columbia River for the United States.

Name of the important feature in the Oregon Country: _____

1.
2.
3.
4.
5.
6.
7.
8.
9.
10.
11.
12.
13.

The Panama Canal

Once California and Oregon became part of the United States, the government and businessmen saw the benefit of having a canal through Central America. A canal would make it much easier and faster to travel from the Atlantic to the Pacific than traveling all the way around the southern tip of South America.

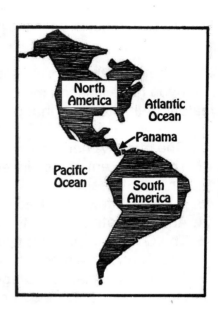

This was not a new idea. In 1850, the United States and England signed a treaty agreeing that neither country would build a canal through Central America without permission of the other. In the 1880s, a French company, which was not part of the treaty, hired Ferdinand de Lesseps, the man who built the Suez Canal, to build a canal through what is now Panama. This project failed, but Americans felt that it was still a good idea and that it was possible to build a canal, so the United States paid the French company for its rights to finish the canal. England gave the United States permission to build the canal if the United States would agree to open the canal to ships of all nations.

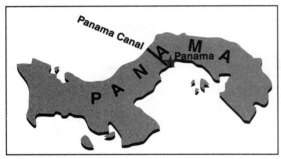

In the early part of the twentieth century, when the United States wanted to build the canal, the Isthmus of Panama belonged to Colombia, a South American country. When Theodore Roosevelt, president of the United States, asked Colombia's permission to build the canal, the Colombian government made so many demands that the United States considered not building the canal in Panama, but choosing another site in Central America. The people in Panama wanted the jobs and the business a canal would bring, so they revolted against Colombia, and with the help of the United States, established the Republic of Panama.

The United States signed a treaty with Panama. In exchange for $10 million and a yearly payment of $250,000, Panama gave the United States a 10-mile-wide strip of land across Panama. This was called the Panama Canal Zone. Between 1904 and 1914, the United States built the Panama Canal, which is 51 miles long, has six locks, and crosses two natural lakes, one of which is 85 feet above sea level. In the 1950s supertankers and other ships became so large that many could not fit through the canal.

The Canal Zone was administered by the United States until 1979. It was then turned over to Panama. Panama agreed to guarantee the neutral operation of the canal.

Panama Canal Quiz

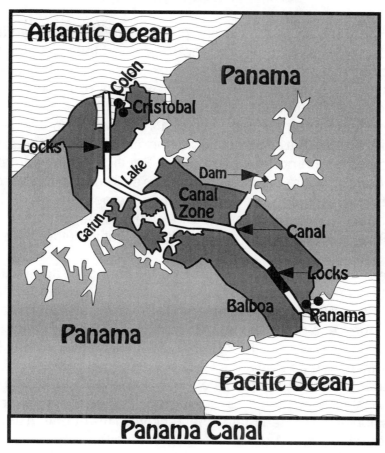

Fill in the blank with the missing word or words.

1. The Panama Canal has _____ locks.

2. The canal was built in Panama to transport goods and people between the _____ and _____ Oceans.

3. The Panama Canal is _____ miles long.

4. In 1850 the United States and _____ signed a treaty agreeing that neither country would build a canal through Central America without the permission of the other.

5. The 10-mile-wide strip of land across Panama is called the Panama Canal _____.

6. At the end of 1979 control of the canal was passed to _____ .

7. Ferdinand de Lesseps is the man who built the _____ .

8. In the early part of the twentieth century, U.S. President _____ asked Colombia's permission to build the canal.

9. If it were not for the canal, ships would need to sail around the tip of _____ to get from the Atlantic Ocean to the Pacific Ocean.

10. The Panama Canal was built between the years of _____ and _____ .

Name:_____ Date: _____

Alaska

The area that is now known as Alaska has played a very important part in the history of the Americas. Thousands of years ago, the Ice Age uncovered land masses that are under water today. One of these land masses connected Alaska to Siberia, and anthropologists believe that the people who populated the Americas were Asians who walked across this land bridge. The American Indians are decendants of these people.

Danish explorer Vitus Bering sighted Alaska in 1741, while on a voyage from Siberia. The Bering Strait, the body of water that separates Asia from North America, was named after him. The Bering Sea, which is part of the northern arm of the Pacific Ocean, was also named after him. James Cook and Frederick William Beechey, two British sailors, also explored this area in the latter part of the eighteenth century and the early part of the nineteenth century. These explorers were not as interested in the land or in settlements as they were in the fur pelts they brought back from their voyages. Russian whalers and fur traders were the first to settle in Alaska on Kodiak Island in 1784.

William H. Seward, who was U.S. Secretary of State during the administrations of Lincoln and Johnson, saw the value of Alaska, Hawaii, and several Caribbean islands and wanted to purchase them for the United States. While congress refused to buy the Caribbean islands or annex Hawaii, they did approve the purchase of Alaska from Russia. In 1867, the United States bought Alaska from Russia for $7,200,000. Many in America thought it was foolish to buy this great frozen land and referred to the transaction as Seward's Folly or Seward's Icebox.

Just 13 years later, however, the discovery of gold began a new gold rush era. Thousands of people poured into Alaska, hoping to become rich. The gold rush eventually subsided, and Alaska was a possession of the United States that received little attention until Congress approved the Alaska Statehood Act in 1958. Alaska officially became the forty-ninth state in 1959. In 1968, oil was discovered at Prudhoe Bay, and nine years later the first oil flowed through the 800-mile-long Alaskan Pipeline. It is estimated there is enough oil to fill 10 billion barrels.

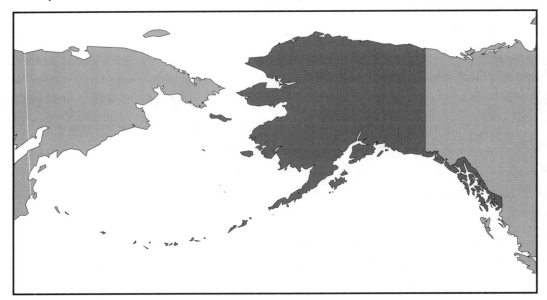

Using the map shown above, locate and label the following: Alaska, Canada, Russia, Bering Strait, Mt. McKinley, Anchorage, Juneau, Barrow, Valdez, Kodiak Island, Alaska Peninsula, Fairbanks, and Nome.

Name:_____ Date: _____

Hawaii

About 2,000 miles away from the mainland of the United States lies Hawaii, the last state to be admitted to the Union. Hawaii is not just one island, but 130 islands that were created by volcanoes millions of years ago. Only eight of these islands are very large, and only seven are regularly inhabited. Hawaii is the largest island of the group, and Oahu, where the capital, Honolulu, is located, is the most heavily populated. The other main islands are Maui, Kahoolawe, Kauai, Lanai, Molokai, and Niihau.

Polynesian voyagers from the Marquesas Islands and Tahiti were the first Hawaiian settlers. Europeans did not report visiting the islands until 1778 when Captain James Cook, an English explorer, arrived and named the Islands the Sandwich Islands, after the Earl of Sandwich. Foreigners began trading with the inhabitants of the Hawaiian Islands, and people from many different cultures moved to the Islands.

For many years, Hawaii was ruled by a monarchy. In 1893, Queen Liliuokalani, was overthrown, and the United States annexed Hawaii in 1898 during the Spanish-American War. Two years later, in 1900, Hawaii was constituted a U.S. territory. In 1950, Hawaii drafted a constitution, and in 1959, it became a state.

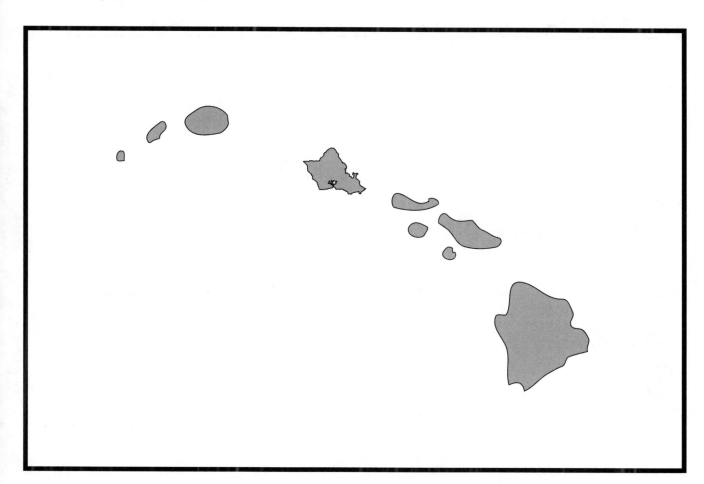

On the map shown above, label the islands: Hawaii, Oahu, Maui, Kahoolawe, Kauai, Lanai, Molokai, and Niihau. Also find and label Honolulu, Pearl Harbor, and Mauna Loa.

Name:_____ Date:_____

Identifying States by Their Shapes

Can you identify the various states of the United States by their shapes? Shown below are the individual states. Write their names underneath each. The sizes of the states are not proportional.

1._____ 2._____ 3._____ 4._____ 5._____

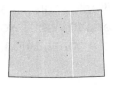   

6._____ 7._____ 8._____ 9._____ 10._____

11._____ 12._____ 13._____ 14._____ 15._____

16._____ 17._____ 18._____ 19._____ 20._____

    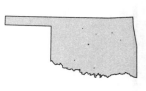

21._____ 22._____ 23._____ 24._____ 25._____

74

Name:_____ Date:_____

Identifying States by Their Shapes (continued)

26._____ 27._____ 28._____ 29._____ 30._____

31._____ 32._____ 33._____ 34._____ 35._____

36._____ 37._____ 38._____ 39._____ 40._____

41._____ 42._____ 43._____ 44._____ 45._____

46._____ 47._____ 48._____ 49._____ 50._____

Slavery in America

Slavery in the Americas began just 25 years after Columbus made his first voyage in 1492. The Native Americans who welcomed the Spaniards when they arrived were killed or forced to work as slaves on plantations the Spanish established. African slaves were brought to Virginia in 1619. Although we generally think of slavery as being a southern practice, at the time of the Revolutionary War, there was slavery in every state. After the Revolutionary War, when the United States was being formed, most people understood that slavery was wrong and should be stopped. In fact, just 20 years after the U.S. Constitution was adopted, a law was passed making it illegal to import slaves from Africa. While this law was a step in the right direction, it did nothing to stop slavery. The country had enough slaves to do all of the work needed on the huge plantations. The owners of these plantations also had a steady supply of new slaves, because the children born of the slaves would also become slaves.

Although slavery was originally practiced in every state, it was mainly a regional issue. The northern states had many factories and relied on skilled workers. The white workers did not want to compete with slaves who would work for nothing. With slaves working for nothing, white workers would have trouble getting jobs and would not be paid very much. On the other hand, the South did not have many factories or workers. There were huge farms or plantations that relied on slaves to do most of the work.

THE MISSOURI COMPROMISE

In 1819, the number of states with slaves was the same as the number of states that did not have slaves. There were 11 states that were called *free states* since there were no slaves, and there were 11 states that were called *slave states*. This was the year that Missouri wanted to be admitted as a state. The question was, should it be a free state or a slave state? This question became a hotly debated subject in Congress. The North was afraid that since Missouri was part of the Louisiana Purchase, that if it were admitted as a slave state, then all of the other states to be formed out of this territory would also be slave states. Southerners felt differently. They said that since many Southerners had already settled in Missouri and had slaves, the federal government had no right to take the slaves away from them. Finally, a compromise on the part of both sides was reached. It was called the Missouri Compromise of 1820. The compromise had the following provisions:

1. Slavery would be allowed in Missouri.
2. Slavery would be forbidden north of the line across the Louisiana Purchase that extended from the upper tip of Texas to the bottom of Missouri (the 36° 30′ line of latitude).
3. Slavery would be permitted south of this line.

When Missouri was admitted as a slave state, Maine was admitted as a free state. So the balance between slave and free states remained the same.

THE COMPROMISE OF 1850

In spite of the Missouri Compromise, disagreements concerning slavery continued. Americans continued their push westward. Some went to California and Texas. Many who went to Texas took their slaves with them. California and Texas were Spanish possessions, but Mexico became independent and claimed this area. However, those living in Texas did not want to be part of Mexico, they wanted to be independent, too. This led to a war, and 10 years after Texas became a Republic, it was admitted as a slave state, since it was south of the Missouri Compromise Line. A few years later in 1848, gold was discovered in California. The population of California grew very quickly and the question of whether California should be a slave state or a free state was raised once again.

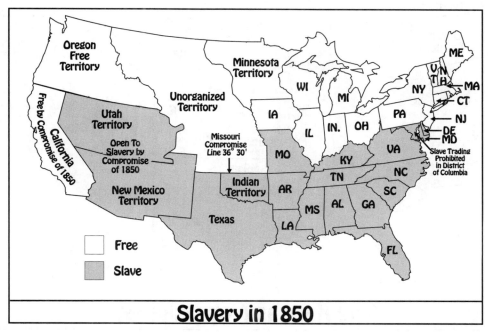

Slavery in 1850

The debate over slavery continued. The South wanted more of the area won from Mexico to be slave states. They threatened to leave the United States and form another United States of the South. The North, of course, disagreed. In 1850, Henry Clay devised a compromise plan to settle the issue. The plan was called a compromise because each side got some things it wanted. Among other things, the Compromise of 1850, as it came to be known, had four provisions:

1. California was to be admitted as a free state.
2. Slave trade—but not slavery—was to be prohibited in the District of Columbia.
3. The new land acquired from Mexico was to be organized into two territories—New Mexico and Utah—and Congress was not to decide if these territories should be slave or free. The people who settled these territories would decide for themselves when they asked to become a state. This was called **popular sovereignty**. The compromise was passed by Congress.
4. A new fugitive slave law was passed. Hiding or helping a slave escape was punishable by a fine and imprisonment.

THE KANSAS-NEBRASKA ACT

In 1853, President Franklin Pierce promised that the Compromise of 1850 would be strictly enforced and that the slavery problem had been solved. In a matter of only a few weeks, however, that changed. Senator Stephen A. Douglas from Illinois introduced a bill to Congress to create two new territories from part of the Louisiana Purchase just west of Missouri and Iowa. The names of these two territories were to be Kansas and Nebraska. The bill also said that the people in these two new territories should be able to vote if they wanted slavery or not. This violated the Missouri Compromise of 1820, which said that any new state admitted that was west or north of Missouri had to be a free state. Douglas said that the Compromise of 1850, which included popular sovereignty, took the place of the Missouri Compromise. After a difficult fight in the Congress, the Kansas-Nebraska Act passed and became law. Nebraska became a free state without much problem, but there was bitter fighting and conflict in Kansas before it voted to be a free state.

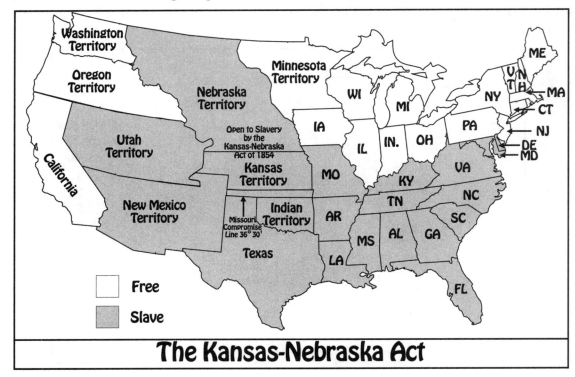

The Kansas-Nebraska Act

Slavery Leads to War

Some people predicted that if Abraham Lincoln were elected president of the United States in 1860, the Southern states would secede from the Union. Many Northerners did not take these predictions seriously, but when Abraham Lincoln was elected, this is exactly what happened. The first state to leave the Union was South Carolina. Soon after South Carolina declared itself "an independent commonwealth," six other cotton producing states—Alabama, Florida, Georgia, Mississippi, Louisiana, and Texas—also seceded. In February,1861, representatives of the states that had left the Union met in Montgomery, Alabama, and adopted a provisional constitution for the newly-formed group called the **Confederate States of America**. Jefferson Davis was elected president, and Alexander H. Stephens was elected vice president of the Confederacy. President Davis then appointed a Cabinet.

The Confederacy hoped the remaining eight slave states would secede and become part of the newly-organized Confederacy, but only four—Arkansas, Tennessee, North Carolina, and Virginia—separated themselves from the Union once the war began. The other four states—Delaware, Kentucky, Maryland, and Missouri—were called **border states**. The border states were slave states located on the border between the Confederate states and the free states in the Union.

Not everyone in the South wanted to secede. Texas Governor Sam Houston opposed succession. Even Alexander H. Stephens who was elected vice president of the Confederacy originally opposed succession. Forty counties in Virginia felt so strongly the Union should be preserved that they held their own constitutional convention after Virginia had seceded and decided to form a new state called West Virginia and become part of the Union.

Many believe that the War Between the States was fought to abolish slavery. This is not quite true. While the issue of slavery caused the Southern states to secede, which eventually led to war, the North did not go to war to abolish slavery. It fought to preserve the Union. By the same token, the South did not go to war to defend slavery. It was fighting for states' rights. The South felt each state had the right to secede and to govern itself.

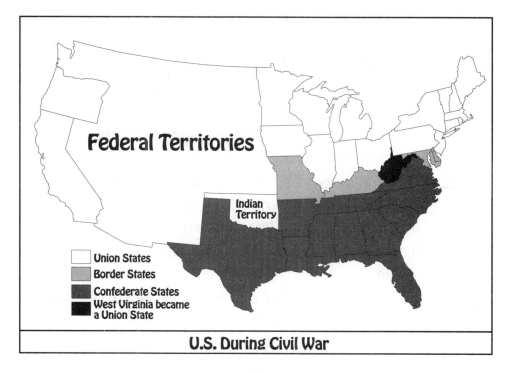

Federal Territories

Indian Territory

☐ Union States
▨ Border States
▨ Confederate States
■ West Virginia became a Union State

U.S. During Civil War

79

Slavery Quiz

Name: _____ Date: _____

Shown below are a number of sentences. Some are true and some are false. If the sentence is true, write the word "true" in front of the sentence. If the sentence is false, write a term that could replace the term written in bold type to make the sentence true.

_____ 1. **Spanish** slaves were brought to Virginia in 1619.

_____ 2. The South did not have many **factories**.

_____ 3. At the time of the **Civil** War, there was slavery in every state.

_____ 4. Slavery in the Americas began just 25 years after **Balboa** made his first voyage in 1492.

_____ 5. As a result of the Missouri Compromise, **Missouri** was admitted as a slave state.

_____ 6. As a result of the Missouri Compromise, **Maine** was admitted as a free state.

_____ 7. Twenty years after the U.S. Constitution was adopted, a law was passed making it illegal to import slaves from **Asia**.

_____ 8. The **Southern** states had many factories.

_____ 9. In **1819,** the number of states with slaves was the same as the number of states that did not have slaves.

_____ 10. The south had huge farms or **plantations**.

_____ 11. Children born of the slaves would also become **slaves**.

_____ 12. In 1848, gold was discovered in **Utah**.

_____ 13. Some people predicted that if **Jefferson Davis** was elected president of the United States, the Southern states would secede.

_____ 14. Stephen A. Douglas from Illinois introduced a bill in Congress to create two new territories—**Kansas** and Nebraska.

_____ 15. The North was afraid if Missouri was admitted as a slave state, then all of the other states formed out of the **Gadsden** Purchase would also be slave states.

_____ 16. In February 1861, representatives from states that had left the Union met in Montgomery, Alabama, and adopted a constitution for the **Consolidated** States of America.

_____ 17. Texas became a **Republic** when it won its independence from Mexico.

_____ 18. Texas was admitted as a slave state since it was south of the **Missouri** Compromise Line.

Name: _____ Date: _____

_____ 19. The first state to leave the **Confederacy** was South Carolina.

_____ 20. Alexander H. Stephens was vice president of the **Confederacy**.

_____ 21. According to the Missouri Compromise, slavery was forbidden north of the line across the Louisiana Purchase that extended from the upper tip of Texas to the bottom of **Texas**.

_____ 22. According to the Compromise of 1850, **California** was to be admitted as a free state.

_____ 23. According to the Compromise of 1850, slave trade—but not slavery— was to be prohibited in the **District of Columbia**.

_____ 24. According to the Compromise of 1850, The new land acquired by the war with Mexico was to be organized into two territories—New Mexico and **Old Mexico**.

_____ 25. According to the Compromise of 1850, the question of slavery in New Mexico and Utah was to be decided by the **governor**.

_____ 26. The term called "**popular sovereignty**," refers to letting residents decide if a state should have slavery.

_____ 27. As a result of the Compromise of 1850, a new **compromise** law was passed.

_____ 28. Some people complained that the Compromise of 1850 violated the **Missouri** Compromise of 1820.

_____ 29. Forty counties in Virginia felt so strongly the Union should be preserved that, after Virginia had seceded, they formed a new state called **West Virginia** and became part of the Union.

_____ 30. There was bitter fighting and conflict in **Nebraska** before it voted to be a free state.

_____ 31. **Northerners** felt they were fighting the Civil War to preserve the Union.

_____ 32. The **South** felt they were fighting for states' rights.

The Transcontinental Railroad

On May 10, 1869, the transcontinental railroad was completed and the country celebrated. Before the transcontinental railroad was finished, it took several months of dangerous travel to reach the west. Travelers who wished to go to California risked their lives to either sail around Cape Horn or to plod over land across deserts, mountains, and Indian territory. After completion of the railroad, travelers could make the trip in a week and a half. Not only was the trip faster, safer, and more comfortable, but passengers could also shoot buffalo out of the window of the train to pass the time. This was one factor that almost led to the extinction of the buffalo.

The importance of the transcontinental railroad was not only that it made travel faster between the coasts, but it also united the country. The lure of the gold mines of California and the desire for the seemingly endless rich land of the west was only a dream for most Americans. The transcontinental railroad made that dream possible. The completion of the railroad was an enormous task and seemed to bring all Americans together. This was especially important because of the divisions between the North and the South. The War Between the States had been fought just a few years before. But now the country that had been divided was for the first time in its history united.

The idea of a transcontinental railroad system was first suggested by newspapers in the 1830s. Although Congress did improve many railroads that extended the range of travel to the west, the location of a transcontental railroad was hotly debated before the Civil War. The North obviously felt the railroad should run through the northern part of the country. The South felt just as strongly that the railroad should run through the South. In 1862, during the war, Congress decided the transcontinental railroad should be built between Omaha, Nebraska, and Sacramento, California. Congress chose the Central Pacific Railroad to lay the tracks from California and the Union Pacific Railroad to build from the eastern part of the railroad. The government agreed to pay each company for every mile of track that was laid. So there was great competition between the two companies to work as fast as they could. The more track they laid, the more money they made.

The Central Pacific hired thousands of workers from China to perform the many dangerous jobs required. The workers were paid $1 a day plus food and worked 12-hour shifts. The mountains were so rugged that the crews sometimes laid only a foot of track a day. The Union Pacific had a more diverse group of workers. They hired many European immigrants such as Germans, Dutch, Irish, and Czechoslovakians, but they also hired Civil War veterans and recently-freed slaves. They also worked 12-hour shifts, just like the Central Pacific workers.

On May 10, 1869, the Central Pacific and the Union Pacific met at Promontory Point, Utah, to complete the United States' first transcontinental railroad. Leland Stanford, the Governor of California and one of the four heads of the Central Pacific Railroad, and Dr. Thomas Durant, the vice president of the Union Pacific, drove a golden spike to connect the two tracks.

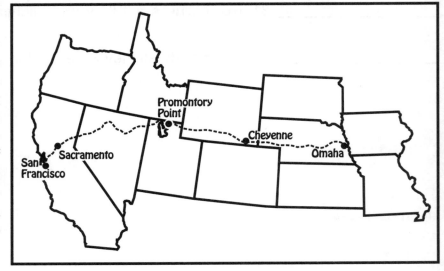

Name: _____ Date: _____

Transcontinental Railroad Quiz

Listed below are a number of definitions associated with railroads. Write the appropriate word opposite each definition. Choose from the words listed at the bottom of the page. Many of the railroad terms are part of our everyday vocabulary today.

1. The foundation for the rails and ties of a railroad _____

2. Where the Union Pacific started to build its railroad westward _____

3. Measuring and placing the rails the proper distance apart _____

4. The company that built the transcontinental railroad from California eastward

   _____

5. A track running beside the main track permitting trains to pass_____

6. Men who smoothed and flattened the road bed _____

7. Where the Union Pacific and Central Pacific rails met_____

8. Long iron nails driven into the ties to secure the track _____

9. The timbers that support the rails_____

10. The company that built the transcontinental tracks from Omaha, Nebraska westward

    _____

11. Fired _____

12. Gravel, slag, or other material used as a road bed_____

13. Tracks within and/or around a city _____

14. A type of locomotive engine _____

15. To replace an employee with less seniority _____

16. The last car at the rear of a freight train _____

17. A structure above the roof of a caboose from which a trainman may see along the train while it is in motion_____

18. Two main tracks, on which the trains run in one direction on one track and in the opposite direction on the other track _____

19. Combustible torches used as a warning signal to other trains _____

20. An employee who oils and greases switches and track equipment _____

21. A railroad detective _____

22. A student telegrapher _____

23. Car with hinged trap doors and inclined floors permitting fast unloading of certain types of material _____

24. A track on a pivot used to turn locomotives or cars onto a special track _____

Ballast , Belt Line, Bump, Caboose, Canned, Central Pacific, Crows Nest, Diesel, Flares, Double Track, Gauging, Grease Monkey, Graders, Gumshoe, Ham, Hopper, Omaha, Promontory Point, Road Bed, Siding, Spikes, Ties, Turntable, Union Pacific

83

Canals

From the earliest recorded time, humans have used travel on water as a cheap, convenient means of transportation. In America, early settlers traveled west in flatboats since there were few roads and those that existed were poorly maintained. Since the boats were large, the pioneers were able to load up all they owned and then float downstream. It was much easier than traveling by wagon. Farmers and businessmen also used the rivers to transport their goods to ports downstream. New Orleans was a popular destination.

However, there were problems with traveling or transporting goods on the rivers. In addition to sandbars, snags, river pirates and Indians, there were rapids and waterfalls. When a boat came to a rapids or a waterfall, it would need to be unloaded, towed around the obstruction, and then reloaded. This problem was solved by building canals around obstructions such as rapids or falls. The first canal was built in Virginia in 1785 and was seven miles long. Afterwards, other canals were built in various parts of the country to link one waterway with another.

The most famous canal was the Erie Canal. It was over 360 miles long and stretched from the Hudson River to Buffalo, New York. When it was finished in 1825, it was possible to travel from New York City to Lake Erie by water. Other canals were built that intersected with each other, making it possible for goods to travel easily between the ports on the Atlantic Ocean to the cities located along the Great Lakes. Eventually canals were built from Lake Erie to intersect major rivers such as the Ohio.

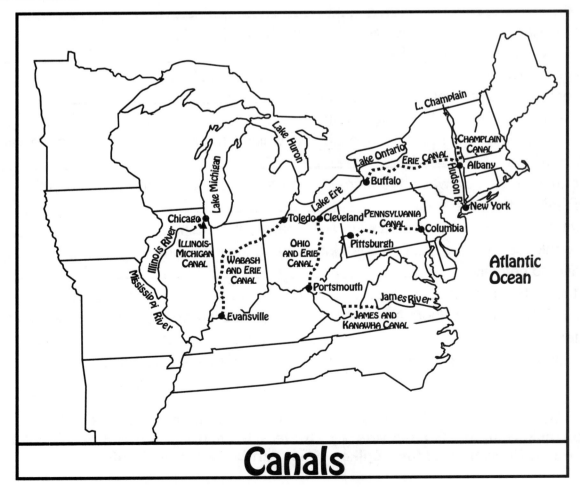

Canals

Name: _____ Date: _____

Famous Ship Canals

The Panama Canal is considered a remarkable achievement. It saves precious sailing time when transporting goods or passengers. Are you aware of some of the other famous canals in the world? Listed below are some of the well-known canals. Answer the questions below.

NAME	LOCATION	LENGTH	YEAR OPENED
Albert	Belgium	80.0*	1939
Amsterdam-Rhine	Netherlands	45.0	1952
Beaumont-Port Arthur	United States	40.0	1916
Houston	United States	50.0	1914
Kiel	Germany	61.3	1895
Panama	Panama	50.7	1914
St. Lawrence Seaway	U.S. and Canada	2,400	1959
Sault Ste. Marie	Canada	1.2	1895
Sault Ste. Marie	United States	1.6	1915
Suez	Egypt	100.6	1869

*miles

Canal Quiz

1. Which canal is the longest?_____

2. How long is it? _____

3. Which canal is the oldest? _____

4. When was it built? _____

5. Which canal is the newest?_____

6. When was it built? _____

7. Which canal is the shortest?_____

8. What is its length? _____

9. Name the canals that go through two countries. _____

_____

10. Name the two countries these canals go through._____

11. What is the name of the canal that is in Belgium?_____

12. What is the name of the famous canal in Egypt? _____

13. In which country is the Kiel Canal? _____

Answer Keys

Ice Age Definitions (page 3)
1. predator
2. musk ox
3. Lake Superior
4. La Brea tar pits
5. moraines
6. Lake Agassiz
7. saber-toothed tiger
8. mastodon
9. Ice Age
10. glaciers
11. Great Lakes
12. Pleistocene Period
13. extinct
14. dinosaurs
15. woolly mammoth
16. corn belt
17. Siberia
18. tusks
19. mammals
20. fang
21. prehistoric
22. armadillo

Route of the First Americans (page 5)

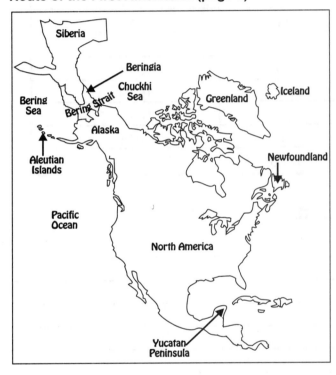

Viking Voyages Map Activity (page 9)

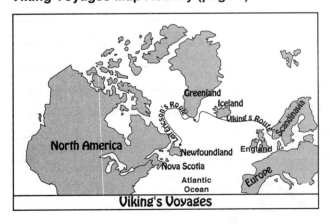

Columbus Quiz (page 11)
1. True
2. Italian
3. ships
4. True
5. True
6. Indians
7. True
8. Asia or the Indies
9. True
10. 1492
11. poor
12. Marco Polo
13. True
14. round
15. India
16. Portugal

Other Early Explorers Quiz (page 16)
1. Italians
2. True
3. True
4. True
5. Sea
6. Portuguese
7. True
8. Stormy Cape
9. True
10. India
11. Dias'
12. True
13. True
14. Columbus
15. True
16. Spain
17. South America
18. True
19. True
20. Ocean
21. Balboa
22. Pacific Ocean
23. Natives
24. True
25. Larger
26. Pacific
27. True
28. True
29. No
30. True

Spanish Explorers Quiz (page 18)
1. Island
2. True
3. True
4. 1565
5. Pizzaro
6. True
7. True
8. De Vaca
9. Cortés
10. True

Spanish Conquistadors Quiz (page 19)
1. the Fountain of Youth
2. Balboa
3. Conquistadors
4. Aztecs
5. Mexico
6. gold
7. Peru
8. Florida
9. Montezuma
10. Peru
11. Florida
12. Galveston, Texas
13. Cabeza de Vaca
14. four
15. Gold
16. Cibola
17. a poor Indian town
18. Mississippi River
19. Mississippi River
20. Indians
21. South Sea
22. the Pacific Ocean
23. Magellan
24. natives
25. stowaway
26. conqueror
27. 45
28. nobleman

French Explorers Puzzle (pages 21–22)

```
 1.  V E R R A Z A N O
 2.              C H A M P L A I N
 3.  M I S S I S S I P P I
 4.              J O L I E T
 5.  M O N T R E A L
 6.                  E R I E
 7.                  O H I O
 8.              C A N A D A
 9.            Q U E B E C
10.                L O U I S I A N A
11.  M I C H I G A N
12.            L A S A L L E
13.                S P A N I S H
14.          N E W F R A N C E
15.              M A R Q U E T T E
16.            C A R T I E R
17.          F R A N C E
```

Famous Explorers (page 25)

Explorer	County	Date	Purpose	Accomplishment
Dias	Portugal	1486	To find an all-water route to Asia	Rounded the tip of Africa
Columbus	Spain	1492	To find a westward route to Asia	Reached America by sailing west from Europe
Cabot	England	1497	To find a westward route to Asia	Laid the basis for English claim to North America
Da Gama	Portugal	1498	To reach India by sea	First European to reach India by the sea route
Vespucci	Spain	1499	Exploration	The explorer after whom the New World was named
Balboa	Spain	1513	Exploration and adventure	Discovered the Pacific Ocean
Magellan	Spain	1519	To find a westward route to Asia	First to circumnavigate the globe
Cortés	Spain	1521	To gain riches and power	Conqueror of the Aztecs and Mexico
Verrazano	France	1524	To claim new lands for France To find a westward route to Asia	Laid basis for French claims in North America
Pizarro	Spain	1531	To gain riches and power	Conquered Peru
Cartier	France	1534	To discover a northwest passage to China	Discovered and explored the St. Lawrence River
De Soto	Spain	1539	To explore Florida and gain riches	Discovered the Mississippi River
Coronado	Spain	1540	To find Cibola, the Seven Cities of Gold	Explored the southwestern part of the United States
Champlain	France	1608	To explore and to find a westward route to Asia	Founded Quebec; was known as the Father of New France
Hudson	Holland	1609	To discover a Northwest Passage to China	Explored the Hudson River
La Salle	France	1682	Exploration and trade	Discovered the Ohio River, explored the Mississippi to its mouth

Who Gets the New World? (page 26)

1. Spain; there was more territory west of the line than east of the line.
2. The people in Brazil speak Portuguese, while most of the rest of South and Central America is Spanish-speaking.

New Spain Quiz (page 28)

1. south
2. cruel
3. St. Augustine
4. farmers
5. True
6. slaves
7. True
8. Christianity or Catholicism
9. True
10. True

Countries That Colonized (pages 33–34)

1. F	11. E	21. D	31. D
2. S	12. F	22. S	32. F
3. D	13. E	23. E	33. D
4. E	14. S	24. F	34. D
5. S	15. E	25. D	35. F
6. E	16. S	26. E	
7. S	17. E	27. S	
8. F	18. F	28. E	
9. E	19. S	29. S	
10. S	20. D	30. F	

Knowing the Original Colonies (page 36)
1. Massachusetts; The northern section is now Maine.
2. New Hampshire
3. Rhode Island
4. Connecticut
5. New York
6. Pennsylvania
7. New Jersey
8. Delaware
9. Maryland
10. Virginia
11. North Carolina
12. South Carolina
13. Georgia

French and Indian War Map and Quiz (page 38)

Name	British Fort	French Fort	Neither	Battle
Niagara		X		X
Duquesne		X		X
Necessity	X			X
Cumberland	X			X
Le Boeuf		X		X
Prequie Isle		X		
Ontario		X		
Venango		X		X
Frontenac		X		X
Crown Point		X		X
Ticonderoga		X		X
William Henry	X			X
Louisburg			X	X
Quebec			X	X
Montreal			X	X

How Well Do You Know Canada? (page 39)

Important Battles of the Revolutionary War (page 42)

Battle	Year	Winner	Importance
Lexington and Concord	1775	Colonists	First battle of the war. Emerson said that at this battle a shot was fired that was "heard round the world."
Bunker Hill	1775	England	Located close to Boston, there were heavy English losses as a result of the battle.
Long Island	1776	England	Fought between the troops of Washington and Howe. It was the first large-scale battle of the war.
Trenton and Princeton	1776-1777	United States	An important early victory in the war. After earlier defeats, this battle restored the morale of the U.S. troops.
Saratoga	1777	United States	Fought in upstate New York. France offered its help. It was a turning point in the war.
Yorktown	1781	United States	Last battle of the war.

Patriots of the American Revolution (page 43)

1. Casimir Pulaski
2. John Adams
3. Patrick Henry
4. Crispus Attucks
5. Molly Pitcher
6. Betsy Ross
7. Thomas Jefferson
8. John Paul Jones
9. Benjamin Franklin
10. Paul Revere
11. John Hancock
12. Martha Washington
13. Samuel Adams
14. George Washington
15. James Otis
16. Robert Morris
17. Marquis de Lafayette
18. Thomas Paine
19. George Rogers Clark
20. Baron Friedrich von Steuben
21. Deborah Samson
22. Johann de Kalb

Separated by a Common Language (page 44)

1. Movie theatre
2. Americans
3. Apartment
4. Drop out
5. Police car
6. Expensive
7. Quarrel
8. Call
9. Bathroom
10. Battery
11. Babysitter
12. Can
13. Carpenter
14. Cookie
15. Counterclockwise
16. Dessert
17. Diaper
18. Elevator
19. Faucet
20. Soccer
21. Electrician
22. Flashlight
23. French fries
24. Guy
25. Car hood
26. Private school
27. Jail
28. Ladybug
29. Lawyer
30. Leash
31. License plate
32. Like
33. Mail
34. Appointment book
35. Pharmacist
36. Drunk
37. Policeman
38. Popsicle
39. Intermission
40. Aluminum

Separated by a Common Language (cont.) (page 55)

41. Rent
42. Boy
43. Arrest
44. Stupid
45. Suspenders
46. Trunk
47. TV
48. Two weeks
49. Vacation
50. Very
51. Yard
52. Sidewalk

War of 1812 Quiz (page 46)

1. Jefferson
2. Britain
3. True
4. New Orleans
5. Jackson
6. True
7. True
8. Star-Spangled Banner
9. True
10. white

The Star-Spangled Banner Quiz (pages 47–48)

1. And the rockets' red glare
2. Gave proof thro' the night
3. by the dawn's early light,
4. the land of the free
5. the bombs bursting in air,
6. Whose broad stripes and bright stars
7. Oh, say, can you see,
8. Oh, say, does that star-spangled banner yet wave
9. the home of the brave?
10. O'er the ramparts we watch'd
11. thro' the perilous fight,

War With Mexico Puzzle (page 53)

1. MEXICO
2. ALAMO
3. LOUISIANAPURCHASE
4. RIOGRANDE
5. FRENCH
6. MEXICO
7. SPAIN
8. TEXAS
9. GADSDEN
10. MONROE
11. JACKSON
12. STAR
13. FLORIDA
14. SANTAANNA
15. DAVYCROCKETT

Are You From Virginia? (page 56)

1. G	6. M	11. N	16. C	21. M
2. C	7. V	12. G	17. N	22. C
3. M	8. G	13. V	18. G	23. V
4. V	9. V	14. C	19. C	24. V
5. C	10. C	15. N	20. M	25. V

Famous Native Americans (page 58)

1. Red Cloud—A Sioux chief who fought U.S. occupation of Wyoming.
2. Sitting Bull—A Sioux leader born in present-day South Dakota. He resisted the efforts of the United States to take the Sioux and put them on reservations. He fought and defeated General Custer. Although he was offered amnesty, he was arrested and shot and killed.
3. Crazy Horse—A Sioux chief who also resisted Indian confinement to reservations. He and Sitting Bull defeated Custer in the Battle of Little Bighorn. He eventually surrendered and was killed in a fight with his captors.
4. Sacajewea—A Shoshone Indian woman, who along with her Canadian trapper husband, was hired as an interpreter and guide for Lewis and Clark.
5. Will Rogers—A humorist and writer. He worked in vaudeville and in movies. He is famous for his monologues and newspaper articles making fun of politicians.
6. Jim Thorpe—Many feel that he was one of the greatest athletes of the century. He was an excellent baseball player, football player, and track and field athlete. He won both the pentathlon and the decathlon in the 1912 Olympics.
7. Pocahontas—Befriended the English settlers. It is said she saved the life of Captain John Smith. She married John Rolfe.

Identify States Developed from the Northwest Territory (page 59)

1. Ohio - Columbus
2. Indiana - Indianapolis
3. Illinois - Springfield
4. Michigan - Lansing
5. Wisconsin - Madison
6. Minnesota - St. Paul

Identify States Developed From the Louisiana Purchase (page 61)

Teacher check.

Lewis and Clark Quiz (page 63)

1. Louisiana Purchase
2. True
3. Missouri
4. True
5. Pike
6. Mississippi
7. Mandan
8. 1804
9. $2\frac{1}{2}$
10. southwestern

Growth of the United States Quiz (page 65)

1. California—Mexican cession as a result of the War with Mexico in 1848
2. Florida—Purchased from Spain in 1819
3. Washington—By treaty with Great Britain 1846
4. Arkansas—Louisiana Purchase in 1803
5. Texas—Annexed in 1845 and the rest as a result of the War with Mexico in 1848
6. Louisiana—Louisiana Purchase in 1803
7. Nebraska—Louisiana Purchase in 1803
8. Idaho—By treaty with Great Britain in 1846
9. Utah—Mexican cession as a result of the War with Mexico in 1848
10. South Dakota—Louisiana Purchase in 1803

11. east to west
12. Louisiana Purchase
13. Revolutionary
14. France
15. Mexican-American
16. True
17. True
18. Idaho
19. Spanish
20. Texas
21. Minnesota
22. Alaska
23. Hawaii
24. Louisiana Territory
25. after

Which Trail Would You Take? (page 67)

1. Oregon Trail
2. Oregon Trail, California Trail
3. Santa Fe Trail
4. Santa Fe Trail, Desert Trail
5. Oregon Trail, California Trail
6. Oregon Trail
7. Santa Fe Trail, Desert Trail
8. Oregon Trail, California Trail
9. Santa Fe Trail, Desert Trail or Old Spanish Trail
10. Santa Fe Trail, Desert Trail

Oregon Country Puzzle (page 69)

1. CLARK
2. POLK
3. CALIFORNIA
4. UTAH
5. MOUNTAINS
6. BRITAIN
7. SPAIN
8. WASHINGTON
9. RUSSIA
10. LEWIS
11. VANCOUVER
12. UNITED
13. GRAY

Panama Canal Quiz (page 71)

1. six
2. Atlantic, Pacific
3. 51
4. England
5. Zone
6. Panama
7. Suez Canal
8. Theodore Roosevelt
9. South America
10. 1904, 1914

Alaska (page 72)

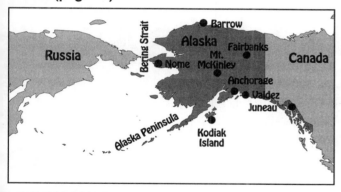

Hawaii (page 73)

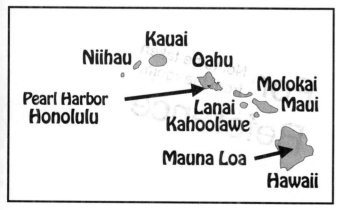

Identifying States By Their Shapes (pages 74–75)

1. Hawaii
2. Georgia
3. Florida
4. Delaware
5. Connecticut
6. Colorado
7. California
8. Arkansas
9. Arizona
10. Alaska
11. Alabama
12. Montana
13. Missouri
14. Mississippi
15. Minnesota
16. Michigan
17. Massachusetts
18. Louisiana
19. Kentucky
20. Kansas
21. Iowa
22. Indiana
23. Illinois
24. Idaho
25. Oklahoma
26. Oregon
27. Pennsylvania
28. Ohio
29. North Dakota
30. North Carolina
31. New York
32. New Mexico
33. New Jersey
34. New Hampshire
35. Nevada
36. Nebraska
37. Wyoming
38. Wisconsin
39. West Virginia
40. Washington
41. Virginia
42. Vermont
43. Utah
44. Texas
45. Rhode Island
46. South Dakota
47. Maine
48. South Carolina
49. Maryland
50. Tennessee

Slavery Quiz (pages 80–81)

1. African
2. True
3. Revolutionary
4. Columbus
5. True
6. True
7. Africa
8. Northern
9. True
10. True
11. True
12. California
13. Abraham Lincoln
14. True
15. Louisiana
16. Confederate
17. True
18. True
19. Union
20. True
21. Missouri
22. True
23. True
24. Utah
25. residents
26. True
27. Fugitive Slave
28. True
29. True
30. Kansas
31. True
32. True

Transcontinental Railroad Quiz (page 83)
1. Road Bed
2. Omaha, Nebraska
3. Gauging
4. Central Pacific
5. Siding
6. Graders
7. Promontory Point, Utah
8. Spikes
9. Ties
10. Union Pacific
11. Canned
12. Ballast
13. Belt Line
14. Diesel
15. Bump
16. Caboose
17. Crows Nest
18. Double Track
19. Flares
20. Grease Monkey
21. Gumshoe
22. Ham
23. Hopper
24. Turntable

Canal Quiz (page 85)
1. St. Lawrence Seaway
2. 2,400 miles.
3. Suez Canal
4. 1869
5. St. Lawrence Seaway
6. 1959
7. Sault Ste. Marie, Canada
8. 1.2 miles
9. St. Lawrence Seaway and Sault Ste. Marie
10. Canada and the United States
11. Albert
12. Suez
13. Germany